AULD LANG SYNE

AULD LANG SYNE

SECOND SERIES

MY INDIAN FRIENDS

BY

THE RIGHT HON. PROFESSOR. F. MAX MULLER
AUTHOR OF "THE SCIENCE OF LANGUAGE". ETC.

GYAN

Published by

GYAN

Gyan Publishing House
5, Ansari Road
Daryaganj, New Delhi-110002
Phone: 011-47034999, 9811692060
E-mail: books@gyanbooks.com

Distribution Network
gyanbooks.com
India, USA, Canada, UK, Australia, France

ISBN : 978-81-212-3791-8 (PB)
First Published, 1899

2nd Impression 2020

Printed at: Gyan Press, Delhi.

Auld Lang Syne
Author: F. Max Muller

PREFACE

HERE follows the second volume of my *Auld Lang Syne*. In some cases my recollections go back very far, and, after a lapse of nearly seventy years, they may not always be so fresh as they ought to be. It is very strange, on looking back to the various stations through which we have passed in our journey through this life, to find how much our own fate has depended on our surroundings and on circumstances over which we ourselves could not possibly have had any control. Our friends, nay even our enemies, seem to form part of our life, and thus it has come to pass that instead of writing my own life, I have almost unconsciously come to write about my friends rather than about myself. As to enemies, if indeed I ever had any, I prefer to be silent, for it is difficult to be quite fair in speaking of them, and we seldom know, till it is too late, what real benefactors they have been to us. Scholars, who on questions of scholarship differ from us as we differ from them, should never be counted as personal enemies, if only they are truthful and straightforward, and if otherwise, is it not best here also to follow the old rule, *De mortuis nihil nisi bonum?* But with regard to my friends and acquaintances, the older I grow, the more I feel how much I have owed and still owe to them, nay, how often the whole stream of my life has been turned East or West by a word or two spoken by a friend at the right moment, just as a whole train may be turned by the mere touch of a handle by the pointsman.

The first volume of my *Auld Lang Syne* contained recollections of musicians, poets, crowned heads, and beggars, such as had not entirely vanished from the *camera obscura* of my memory. The present volume is chiefly devoted to my *Indian Friends*, and to certain events that first led my attention to India. Though I have had but visions of the rivers, the mountains, the valleys, the forests, and the men and women of India, having never been allowed to visit that earthly paradise, I have known for many years the beauties of its literature, the bold flights of its native philosophy, the fervid devotion of its ancient religion, and these together seem to me to give a much truer picture of what India really was, and is still meant to be in the history of the world, than the Bazaars of Bombay, or the Durbars of Râjahs and Mâharâjahs at Delhi. Of course, I shall be told that my picture of India is purely ideal, but an ideal portrait may sometimes be truer than even a photograph, and, though I trust that my facts on the whole are right, I shall always feel most grateful, if any facts are pointed out to me which either contradict or modify my own judgments.

India has never had full justice done to it, and when I say this I think not only of ancient, but of modern India also. And though it can easily be seen that my chief interest lies with ancient India, it should be remembered that in no other country is the past still so visibly present as in that southernmost home of the ancient family of Aryan speech. There may be more historical monuments, reminding us of the past, in Greece and Italy. But life, with its religion, philosophy, and literature, has completely changed there, and we look in vain for a Socrates or Plato on the steps of the Parthenon, or for a Cato or Cæsar among the lonely columns of the Forum. In India, on the contrary, the religion of the Veda is by no means entirely extinct. Not long ago even one of the old magnificent Vedic sacrifices, the Agnish*t*oma, was performed at Benares with all its pristine array. The old epic poems are still recited by the Pâ*th*akas of the country, and some of the old philosophies are flourishing in native Colleges, such as Nuddea, so that men of the present day, such as Gaurî-*sam*kara, the Prime Minister of Bhavnagar, and the Yogin Râmak*r*ish*n*a, bring back to us in full reality the Rishis and Yogins of a thousand or two thousand years ago.

What seems to me to prevent a full appreciation of the intellectual achievements of ancient and medieval India is that they are mostly looked upon, as we look on the prodigies in our exhibitions, as simply curious. Now, we should never say that Plato and Aristotle were curious. We take them far more seriously. We look upon them as our equals, nay as our teachers. It cannot surely be the brown skin that keeps us from feeling the same sympathy and paying the same homage to the poets and philosophers of ancient India, and that prevents even at the present day any real friendship between the best sons of India and England? That brown skin may at first cause a feeling of strangeness, but I know how easily that feeling can be and has been overcome, and, judging from my own limited experience, I can truly say that there is behind that warm and almost Italian colour of the Âryas of India the same warm heart, the same trust, and the same love as under the white skin of Europeans. Real friendship between the rulers and the ruled in India ought to be no impossibility; it has existed again and again; only it should no longer be the exception, but the rule.

If the account of my Indian Friends, which I give in this volume, should serve here and there to overcome that feeling of strangeness and lead to real trust between the two most distant members of the noble family of Aryan speech, I should indeed feel amply rewarded.

I could not well pass over, as belonging by right to the circle of my friends and acquaintances, the ancient Rishis of the Veda, call them Dîrghatamas, Vasish*th*a, or any other name, and in order to show what these ancient poets were really like, I have ventured to add metrical translations of a few of their hymns, celebrating the matutinal procession of their bright Devas or gods. For these I have to crave the indulgence of my critics. These poets were the first to call me to India, and I have never regretted having followed their call, as far as other calls allowed me to do so. They have revealed to me a whole world of thought of which no trace existed anywhere else, and they have helped me to throw the first faint rays of light and reason on perhaps the darkest period in the history of religion, philosophy, and mythology. That period, which I should like to call the *Etymological*, will, I doubt not, become illuminated hereafter by a flood of light from the same source. The present generation of Vedic students could naturally be that of pioneers only, but they may fairly say *In magnis et voluisse sat est*, or in Sanskrit, Yatne k*ri*te yadi na sidhyati, ko-tra dosha*h*!

F. M. M.

Oxford, *May* 1, 1899.

CONTENTS

AULD LANG SYNE

MY INDIAN FRIENDS

I

MY FIRST ACQUAINTANCE WITH INDIA

How I fell in love with India is a very old, and a very long story. We have all read of young knights who in a dream had a vision of a beautiful princess, and who did not rest until they had found her, delivered her, and, after many hard fights with giants and monsters, carried her home in triumph. I had such a vision of India when I was not yet ten years old. It may seem passing strange that a little boy in a small town of Germany should as far back as 1833 have dreamt of India. Few people would know that small town in which he lived. However, if they will look on

NOTE.—In Sanskrit words an italic *k* should be pronounced like English "ch" in church, italic *g* like "j" in join. Thus, mle*kk*ha, or, as some used to spell it, mlechchha, should be pronounced like mlêcha. Proper names, however, and Oriental words that have already a recognised spelling in English, have mostly been left unchanged.

the map of Germany, somewhere between the 12th and 13th degrees of longitude and the 51st and 52d degrees of latitude, they will find *Dessau*, the capital of the Duchy of Anhalt. It lies on the road from Leipzig to Magdeburg, and in these days of railways people often pass it on their way to Berlin. I have never been a very superstitious man, and have never believed in ghosts or spirits, in table-turnings or spirit-rappings, in visions or apparitions; in fact, in anything that can strike the material senses, and yet pretends to be immaterial, and has nothing to strike with. This is the whole problem of ghosts in a nutshell. If ghosts are immaterial, they cannot strike our eyes, or tickle our ears. They could not even have a sulphurous smell. If, on the contrary, they are material, they are not ghosts. But this by the way. But though an unbeliever in ghosts, I have not been able to withhold my belief from coincidences, strange coincidences, which we have to accept in the course of our life without any attempt to account for them. I well remember when I was at school, one of my copybooks had a large picture of Benares on the outside. It was a very rough picture, but I can still see the men, women, and children as they stepped down the ghats to bathe in the waters of the Ganges. That picture caught my fancy and set me dreaming.

What did I know of India at that time? Nothing but that the people were black, that they burnt their widows, and that, in order to get into Paradise, they had first to be mangled under the wheels of the car of Juggernâth. On my picture, however, they were represented looking tall, and, as I thought, beautiful, certainly not like niggers; and the mosques and temples visible on the shores of the river impressed me as even more beautiful and majestic than the churches and palaces at Dessau. Boys will dream dreams, and as I was sitting idle at school dreaming and seeing visions of Benares, instead of doing my copy, I was suddenly taken by the ear by our writing-master, and told to copy several pages containing such names as Benares, Ganges, India, and all the rest, because I had been so idle and had made a very bad copy. This was my first and somewhat painful acquaintance with India, and it led to nothing else at the time. It simply left the memory of a kind of vision, and, if I had not later in life become devoted to the reality of that vision, I should probably never have thought of my copybook again.

It was when I had left school, and had gone to the University of Leipzig in 1841, that my vision, like a *revenant*, appeared again, and assumed then a more tangible and permanent form. I was getting a little tired of Greek and Latin, and the warmed-up cabbage, the *crambe repetita*, of Homer and Horace, when I heard of the foundation of a new chair—a Chair of Sanskrit—and saw lectures on Indian literature advertised by Professor Brockhaus. Here my curiosity was roused at once; I had already had a slight flirtation with Arabic, but now I fell seriously in love with Sanskrit, and became more and more faithless to my first classical love. Professor Brockhaus was an excellent, kind-hearted, and helpful teacher. I began Sanskrit with a will, and, after I had attended his lectures for several semesters at Leipzig, and had read with him such ordinary books as Nala, *S*akuntalâ, and even a little of the Rig-Veda, I went to Berlin to study under Bopp; and then proceeded to Paris, attracted by the fame of Eugène Burnouf.

At that time my desire to see India, as I had seen it in the visions of my schooldays, became very strong. As classical scholars yearn to see Rome or Athens, I yearned to see Benares, and to bathe in the sacred waters of the Ganges. But at that time such a thing was simply out of the question. At that time to go to India seemed to be the privilege of Englishmen only, and it took half a year to get there, and a great deal more money than I could command. The dream of my life to see India face to face has never been realised. When I was young enough, I had not the wherewithal to go there, and when, later in life, I was invited again and again by my Indian friends to go there, I was too old and too much tied down by duties from which there was no escape. Besides, unless I could have stayed in India at least two or three years, could have learned to speak the languages, and come to know the few native scholars still left, it was nothing to me. My India was not on the surface, but lay many centuries beneath it; and as to paying a globe-trotter's visit to Calcutta and Bombay, I might as well walk through Oxford Street and Bond Street. But, though I never stood on the ghats of Benares, and never saw the men, women, and children step down from them into the sacred waters of the Ganges, I have had the good fortune of knowing a number of Indians in Europe, and no doubt some of the best and most distinguished of the sons and daughters of India. I have often been told that I have been misled by these acquaintances, and have taken far too favourable a view of the Indian character; that I had seen the best of India only, but not the worst. But where is the harm? I have seen what the Indian character can be, I have learnt what it ought to be, and I hope what it will be, and though we cannot expect a whole nation of Rammohun Roys, of Debendranâth Tagores, of Keshub Chunder Sens, of Malabâris and Râmabâis, we ought not to neglect them in our estimate of the capabilities of a whole nation.

DVÂRKANÂTH TAGORE.

Indians did not travel so freely fifty years ago as they do now. The crossing of the black water and all its consequences had not then lost its terrors. When, therefore, in the year 1844, a real Hindu made his appearance in Paris, his visit created a great sensation, and filled me with a strong desire to make his acquaintance. He was a handsome man, and, as he took the best suite of apartments in one of the best hotels in Paris, he naturally roused considerable curiosity. I was then attending Professor Burnouf's lectures at the *Collège de France*, and, as the Indian visitor had brought letters of introduction to that great French savant, I too was introduced to the Indian stranger, and soon came to know him well. He was the representative of one of the greatest and richest families in India, Dvârkanâth Tagore, the father of the Maharshi Debendranâth Tagore, who is still alive, and the grandfather of Satyendranâth Tagore, the first successful native candidate for the Indian Civil Service, whom I knew as a young student in England, and who now, after serving his country and his Empress with great distinction for many years, has retired from the service.

Dvârkanâth Tagore was not a Sanskrit scholar, but he was not unacquainted with Sanskrit literature. The first time I saw him was at the *Institut de France*, when Burnouf presented him with a copy of his splendid edition of the Bhagavat-Purâ*n*a. On one side was the Sanskrit text, on the other the French translation, and it was curious to see the Indian placing his delicate brown fingers on the white page with the French translation, and saying with a sigh, "Oh, if I could read that!" One would have expected that his wish would have been to understand the ancient language of his own country; but no, he pined for a better knowledge of French.

He was not an antiquarian, nor a student of his own religion or of the language of his own sacred books. But when he was told by Burnouf what my plans were, and how I had actually copied and collated the MSS. of the Veda at Paris, he took a lively interest in me. He invited me, and I often spent the mornings with him, talking about India and Indian customs. Strange to say, he was devotedly fond of music, and had acquired a taste for Italian and French music. What he liked was to have me to accompany him on the pianoforte, and I soon found that he had not only a good voice, but had been taught fairly well. So we got on very well together. After complimenting him on his taste for Italian music, I asked him one morning to give me a specimen of real Indian music. He sang first of all what is called Indian, but is really Persian music, without any style or character. This was not what I wanted, and I asked whether he did not know some pieces of real Indian music. He smiled and turned away. "You would not appreciate it," he said ; but, as I asked him again and again, he sat down to the pianoforte, and, after striking a few notes, began to play and sing. I confess I was somewhat taken aback. I could discern neither melody, nor rhythm, nor harmony in what he sang ; but, when I told him so, he shook his head and said : "You are all alike ; if anything seems strange to you and does not please you at once, you turn away. When I first heard Italian music, it was no music to me at all ; but I went on and on, till I began to like it, or what you call understand it. It is the same with everything else. You say our religion is no religion, our poetry no poetry, our philosophy no philosophy. We try to understand and appreciate whatever Europe has produced, but do not imagine that therefore we despise what India has produced. If you studied our music as we do yours, you would find that there is melody, rhythm, and harmony in it, quite as much as in yours. And if you would study our poetry, our religion, and our philosophy, you would find that we are not what you call heathens or miscreants, but know as much of the Unknowable as you do, and have seen perhaps even deeper into it than you have!" He was not far wrong.

He became quite eloquent and excited, and to pacify him I told him that I was quite aware that India possessed a science of music, founded, as far as I could see, on mathematics. I had examined some Sanskrit MSS. on music, but I confessed that I could not make head or tail of them. I once consulted Professor H. H. Wilson on the subject, who had spent many years in India and was himself a musician. But he did not encourage me. He told me that, while in India, he had been to a native teacher of music who professed to understand the old books. He had expressed himself willing to teach him, on condition that he would come to him two or three times a week. Then at the end of half a year he would be able to tell him whether he was fit to learn music, whether he was in fact an Adhikârin, a fit candidate, and in five years he promised him that he might master both the theory and the practice of music. That was too much for an Indian civilian who had his hands full of work, and though he learnt many things from Pandits, Professor H. H. Wilson, then, I believe, Master of the Mint and holding several other appointments besides, had to give up all idea of becoming apprenticed for five years to a teacher of music. Dvârkanâth Tagore was much amused, but he quite admitted that five years was the shortest time in which any man could hope thoroughly to master the intricacies of ancient Hindu music, and I too gave up in consequence all hope of ever mastering such texts as the Sangîta-ratnâkara, the Treasury of Symphony, and similar texts, though they have often tempted my curiosity in the library of the East India House.

There is another member of the Tagore family, Râjah Surindro Mohun Tagore, a very liberal patron of Indian music, who has published a great deal about it, but he too has kept aloof from touching on the old science of music that once existed in India, though we know as yet so little of its literature. If we could accept a tradition that has been repeated again and again by Sanskrit scholars, even by men of great learning, such as the late Professor Benfey, we should have to believe that Guido d'Arezzo (about 1000 A.D.) borrowed his gamut from the Arabs, and that they had adopted it from the Persians, who had been the pupils of the Hindus. In itself such a borrowing has nothing incredible in it, for we know that our figures, not excluding the nought, travelled on the same road, from the Indians to the Persians, the Arabs, the Spaniards, and the Italians. It is true also that one of the Indian gamuts consisted of seven notes, and that these notes went by the names *sa, ri, ga, ma, pa, dha, ni,* which were the first syllables of their Sanskrit names. So far, therefore, there is some plausibility. But if it is maintained that these seven syllables were changed in Italian to the well-known *do, re, mi, fa, sol, la, si,* we require some more of real historical evidence of such a change before stating as a fact what is, as yet, a guess only. Gladly as I should claim any merit for the people of India, it seems to me that the differences between the names of the notes of the two gamuts are greater than their similarities. All we can say is that it is possible that we owe our gamut to India, but until more evidence is produced, we cannot say more. If we remember that we owe the nought to that country, mathematicians will be ready to confess that this was one of the greatest discoveries in the history of mathematics and of all the sciences that depend on mathematics, one of the greatest benefits, in fact, that the East has conferred on the West. Whether we owe to India

Beethoven's symphonies is another question, that has yet to wait for an answer.

My Indian friend Dvârkanâth Tagore, though not learned, was very intelligent, and a man of the world. He rather looked down on the Brâhmans, and when I asked him whether he would have to perform penance, or Prâya*s*/*k*itta, after his return to India, he laughed and said, "No. I am all this time feeding a large number of Brâhmans at home, and that is quite penance enough!" The real penance was, of course, the Pa*ñk*agavya, the five products of the cow which the penitent had to swallow before he could be readmitted to his caste; and these products were not only milk, sour milk, and clarified butter, but likewise other products, such as Mûtra and Gomaya. That penance still exists, and many of our Indian visitors have had to undergo it after their return, though at present the five products of the cow are reduced to infinitesimal proportions and swallowed in the shape of a gilded pill.

But if he took a low view of his Brâhmans, he did not show much more respect for what he called the black-coated English Brâhmans. Much as he admired everything English, he had a mischievous delight in finding out the weak points of English society, and particularly of the English clergy. He read a number of English newspapers, political and ecclesiastic, and he kept a kind of black book in which he carefully noted whatever did not redound very much to the honour of any bishops, priests, or deacons. It certainly was a curious collection of every kind of ecclesiastical scandal, and I have often wondered what could have become of it. His son, the saint-like Debendranâth Tagore, the head of the Ârya-Samâj, would hardly make use of such weapons; but his father delighted in the book, and brought it out whenever the question turned on the respective merits of the Indian and the Christian religion. All I could say was that no religion should be judged by its clergy only, whether in Italy, in England, or in India.

Dvârkanâth Tagore lived in a truly magnificent Oriental style while at Paris. The king, Louis Philippe, received him, nay, he honoured him, if I remember right, by his presence and that of his Court at a grand evening party. The room was hung with Indian shawls, then the height of ambition of every French lady. And what was their delight when the Indian Prince placed a shawl on the shoulders of each lady as she left the room.

When in England, Dvârkanâth fulfilled a sacred duty to the memory of Rammohun Roy, the great religious reformer of India, by erecting a tomb over his ashes in the cemetery at Bristol, little thinking that he would soon share his fate, and die like him in a foreign land.

I believe it was his doing also that a new interest was roused in India for the study of the Veda. It was certainly a curious and anomalous state of things that in a country where the Veda was recognised as the highest authority in religion, invested with all the authority of a divine revelation to a greater degree even than the New Testament is in England, this Bible of theirs should never have been printed, and should have been accessible to a small class of priests only, who knew it by heart and possessed a few MSS. of it. Still, so it was; nay, so much had the study of the Veda become neglected that when a prize was offered by the late J. Muir to anyone who would undertake an edition of it, not a single native scholar was willing or able to undertake the task. When, therefore, Dvârkanâth saw that I was quietly preparing an edition of the most important, in fact, the only true Veda, the Rig-Veda, and that I had copied and collated the MSS. which existed in the Royal Libraries at Paris, at Berlin, and elsewhere, and was going to finish my collection in London, he seems to have informed his son, Debendranâth Tagore, of what I was doing at Paris, who, full of interest for religion and religious reform, despatched about the same time four young native students to Benares, in order to enable them to study the Veda under the guidance of the Pandits of that sacred city. One was to learn the Rig-Veda, another the Sâma-Veda, a third the Ya*g*ur-Veda, a fourth the Atharva-Veda. To judge, however, from a letter of Debendranâth Tagore himself, this may have been a mere coincidence. Unfortunately not one of these young Pandits seems ever to have done any independent work in the direction suggested by Debendranâth Tagore.

I may as well state here that I never claimed nor received the very substantial prize offered by J. Muir. Such vague and exaggerated accounts have been spread and even published as to the magnificent *honorarium* paid to me by the late East India Company that I may as well state that, even if I could have carried through the press one sheet per week, after copying, collating, and adding all the references to Sâya*n*a's commentary, I should never have earned more than £200 a year for a work which during more than twenty years of my life occupied nearly all my time. I do not grudge that time, and I shall always feel deeply grateful to some of the Directors of the old Company for having taken so active an interest in what seemed at the time a very useless undertaking. I do not think that the financial position of India has greatly suffered on account of the printing of the Rig-Veda, nay, the expense incurred for it must have been amply recovered, considering how largely the six large quartos have been used for presents to the Râjahs in India and to the Universities and Museums in Europe. Of course it is impossible to make presents without having to pay for them. If people will invent and exaggerate, I may as well tell them that I believe the youngest clerk in the India Office would have declined to work for twenty years at such a salary as I did. And yet I was as happy as a king all the time.

DEBENDRANÂTH TAGORE.

Though I have never seen the son of Dvârkanâth, Debendranâth Tagore, I have had several most interesting letters from him, and I have always felt the deepest sympathy for his noble and unselfish efforts to purify the religion of his countrymen. He was the patron and friend of Keshub Chunder Sen, and, though he was too conservative to be able to follow his young friend in all his reforms, his love for his enthusiastic pupil never ceased. When Keshub Chunder Sen had been forsaken by nearly all his friends, because he allowed the marriage of his daughter with the Mahârâjah of Kuch Behar, when she was a few months under age, the old man remained true to him to the last, and mourned over him at his death-bed as a father would mourn over his only son.

Here is at least one of Debendranâth Tagore's letters to me. I am always ashamed when I print any letters from my Indian friends. They are far too kind, far too complimentary. I know how to make allowance for their warm heart and for their exuberant language, but I am afraid that to people unacquainted with Eastern skies and Eastern hearts, it will naturally seem that such letters ought never to have been published. But what gives so true a picture of a man as a confidential letter?

CHINSURA, via CALCUTTA,
December 27, 1884.

MY DEAR SIR,

I was very glad to receive your letter. It will always give me pleasure to hear from the Pandit of the Far West who has done so much for the language and literature of my country. There are branches of knowledge and art in which the East is deficient, and which she must learn from foreign sources. But there are other things all her own, and even your enlightened countrymen may turn with pleasure and profit to a leaf or two out of the books of the East to learn something new, to get a glimpse of vistas of thought with which they are not familiar. And you, Sir, have done not a little to open out before the world treasures of Oriental wisdom which only the diligence of scholars like you could unfold. By the publication of the Rig-Veda and the Upanishads you have brought within the reach of European scholars the thoughts and aspirations of our ancient Rishis, hitherto hidden in inaccessible manuscripts. And it is to be hoped that the dissemination of the knowledge of our ancient literature will help to cement the bonds of union between the two peoples who, brought up under a common roof, parted from each other and scattered over distant quarters of the globe, again to be brought together under the mysterious decree of Almighty Providence.

You are perhaps not quite right in taking me for a Sannyâsin in the sense of one who has wholly renounced the world. To be in the world, but not of it, is my *beau ideal* of a Sannyâsin, and in that sense I am one. My sons are settled in life and working before my eyes. I take a keen interest in all that goes on far and near, in my domestic circle and outside. My infirm health, however, does not permit me to take an active part in the affairs of the world. So I have settled down for the present in a country house by the banks of the Ganges, far from the din and bustle of the town, and yet not too far to be out of its reach, and my life glides smoothly along like the waves in winter, resigned to His will and ready to quit its mortal coils at His call.

The schism in the Brahmo Samâj is a thing to be regretted, perhaps it may do present harm to the cause. We should have been stronger, if united, but there is no cause for despondency. The seeds have been sown, and they will bear fruit in God's own time. We are but humble seekers of the Truth and humble workers in her cause. We must work and labour each in his own sphere and according to his own light, regardless of consequences. The crowning and fruition of our work rests with God alone, and we may repose our trust in Him for success. Truth will triumph in the end. Satyam eva jayati.

Accept my best thanks for the copy of your Biographical Essays you have so kindly presented to me. It is a very interesting book, and I have read it with the greatest delight. The charitable feeling which you have shown in judging of Keshub Chunder Sen is worthy of your liberality of thought. I received no intimation from my father regarding the publication of the Rig-Veda. It was my own idea to send Pandits to Benares to study the Vedas. The project entirely originated with me, and had no connection with the work you had taken in hand.

Yours sincerely,

DEBENDRANÂTH TAGORE.

Whatever may be thought by others of such a letter, to me it seems a most instructive and characteristic page in the recent history of India. Let us think, first of all, whether there is a single man living in Europe, a man of wealth and high position in his own country, who could have penned such a letter in a foreign language, whether German or Sanskrit. There is hardly a word in it that would have to be altered, and as to the spirit pervading it, no bishop need be ashamed of it. And yet how many people are there even among members of the Indian Civil Service, who would look upon this man as their equal, not to say, as their better?

What he says about the new lessons which even we in England might learn from India, more particularly from the Rig-Veda and the Upanishads, is by no means a mere phrase. He knew quite well what he meant. He was quite sufficiently acquainted with our language, our literature, our philosophy and religion to have a right to say that there are things in those books which are new to us, and might be truly helpful to everybody who strives to solve for himself the many riddles of this world. Let us remember, first of all, that the Rig-Veda is the oldest book of the world. It is older than anything in Greece and Rome, older, as a book, than any book in China, older than the old Persian Avesta, older than Buddhism and its sacred canon, older also than the Old Testament. I know that this last statement will make many people shake their heads, as if the truth and value of a book depended on its age. Is the Old Testament truer than the New, because it is older? Truth is neither young nor old, it is eternal, and history teaches us that the older a religion, the more has it been exposed to deterioration in the hands of priests and no-priests. Ancient ruins are, no doubt, venerable and impressive, but for dwelling in them and for the daily work of life new buildings are better.

No one would say that because the Rig-Veda is the oldest book of the human race—we cannot call cuneiform or hieroglyphic inscriptions, however large they are, books in the ordinary sense of the word—it is therefore the best or the truest. It is on the contrary a record of the childhood of our race, full of childish things, but full also of such unexpected sparks of thought as occasionally startle us from the minds and mouths of babes. The more childish the words of the Rig-Veda are, the more instructive they should prove to us. Where are we to study the origin of religion of the Aryan race to which we ourselves belong by language and thought, if not in the Rig-Veda? Nor does it require much study. Whoever runs may read it on every page. No one doubts now that the gods of the ancient Âryas were representatives of the great phenomena of nature, conceived in the only way in which, in the then state of language and thought, they could be conceived, that is as active and personified. What we should have anticipated, and what in fact was anticipated by philosophers, was fully confirmed by the hymns of the Rig-Veda, which were found to be addressed to the Dawn, the first miracle and the greatest revelation the world has ever seen, though we have learnt to look upon the light of the morning as a matter of course. They were addressed to the morning Sun, the bringer of light and life, to the blue Sky, the gatherer of clouds, the giver of rain and fertility, to the Earth, the Rivers, the Fire, the Storms, and many more.

During the period reflected in the songs of the Rig-Veda, the poets had already made the step from the worship of many gods, the Devas, or the Bright Ones, as they called them, to the recognition of one, but still personal God above all gods, nay, they had purified the concept of that Supreme Being from all that was implied in a male or female personality, and had acknowledged it as neither of the one nor of the other sex, as untrammelled by what personality means with us, as the true, free, and eternal Godhead of which the other gods were but human renderings more or less perfect. We can watch in the Rig-Veda how all these thoughts and conceptions of the Deity arose naturally in the human heart, and there is no other literature in which the genesis of the Divine in the human mind can be so fully and so clearly watched and studied. A record of this theogonic process is surely worth having, and though it naturally holds true of the Aryan race only, it is after all the race to which we ourselves belong, not merely by blood and bones, but, by what is far more important, by language and thought. If we can observe this theogonic process among other races also, whether civilised or uncivilised, a comparison of the different roads that led to God may become most important. Care, however, must be taken not to mix what is heterogeneous. The religions of uncivilised races, whether ancient or modern, but mostly modern, should be studied by themselves, and of course by scholars only, or by those who have at least a knowledge of the grammar of the language in which the religious ideas of such races lie·imbedded. A beginning in this direction has been made, and much may be expected from ethnological studies in the future. Hitherto they have mostly proved amusing only, and without much scientific value, for which the scarcity of materials is answerable far more than the credulity of some of our ethnological students. What is the true value of the theogony of the Aryan race is its historical character, and its continuity which enables us to watch the growth of the concepts of the gods and of God in an unbroken chain till we arrive, chiefly in the Upanishads, at that true conception of the Godhead, free from all limitations, even from that of personality, in the human sense of that word, a stage that had been reached by Greek and Jewish thinkers at Alexandria in the first centuries of Christianity but was soon afterwards hidden again in the clouds of theological anthropomorphism.

It makes no difference whether we ourselves consider this religious development of Aryan thought of the Godhead as true or mistaken. Its real interest is that it has historical reality and that at all events we can learn lessons from it which we can learn nowhere else. It was my desire to gain a direct knowledge of what is preserved in the Rig-Veda of the earliest religious development of our race, and thus to fill a gap which had been felt for many years and deplored by all true scholars, that made me conceive the idea of publishing the text and native commentary of the Rig-Veda; a task not without its difficulties, both scientific and material, for it would otherwise have been undertaken long before.

I have a letter dated August, 1845, now before me from the late Professor Roth, the editor with Professor Boehtlingk of our great Sanskrit Dictionary, where he says, "It is a truly youthful boldness to undertake an edition of the whole of Sâya*n*a's commentary by yourself alone," and he proposes that I should allow him, Dr. Trithen, Dr. Rieu and others to take each a part of the work. In some respects I am sorry now that I did not accept this offer, for the Veda would have appeared sooner. But there were difficulties in this combination, as in most combinations, and being then very youthful and bold, I took the whole work on my own shoulders.

But if my edition of the Rig-Veda helped to usher in quite a new period in Sanskrit scholarship in Europe, it naturally produced an even greater commotion all over India. After all, it was their Bible, and had never been published before during the three or four thousand years of its existence. Attempts were made in various quarters to taboo it, as having been printed by a Mle*kkh*a and with cow's blood; but the book proved itself too strong, it was indispensable, and was soon accepted even by those who at first had placed it under their interdict. The late Dr. Haug sent me a full account of a meeting held by the Brâhmans at Poonah, who, though unwilling at first to touch the book, called an assembly in which a man, not a Brâhman, read out my edition, and all the Brâhmans corrected whatever MSS. they possessed, according to the text as settled in the distant University of Oxford.

RÂJAH RÂDHÂKANTA DEVA.

This brought me into correspondence with many of the leading men both among the conservative and orthodox, and among the progressive and enlightened party in India. At the head of the conservative party stood then a well-known man, Râjah Râdhâkânta Deva, a kind of Indian Lord Shaftesbury. He had distinguished himself by publishing a large thesaurus of the Sanskrit language in seven large quarto volumes, called the *S*abda-Kalpa-druma, the paradise-tree of words. I was highly pleased when I received so valuable a present from the Râjah, and deeply interested in a letter which accompanied it. People in India, even intelligent people, were evidently very much puzzled, how a Mle*kkh*a, as they called all barbarians, or all not twice-born men, could have got hold in the libraries of Germany, France, and England of the *disjecta membra* of their sacred book, how he could have made it out, and actually corrected it. The reforming party naturally rejoiced in the publication of the Veda. But some even of the old orthodox believers in the Veda were highly pleased when I presented to them their venerable Bible. Strange as it may seem to us, such is the power of a long-continued tradition that even the more enlightened among the Hindus, at least at the time of which I am writing, had no kind of doubt as to the divine origin of the Veda. They looked upon it not only as a revelation granted to mankind thousands of years ago, but they believed that it was premundane, that it had existed in the mind of the Supreme Being from all eternity, and had been breathed forth before the beginning of the world. They thought of it, not as a book, but as a revelation handed down from teacher to pupil in an uninterrupted succession.

There existed manuscripts of it, but not very many, and the only way recognised in India of learning the Veda, without destroying its sanctity and efficacy, was to learn it by heart from the mouth of a qualified teacher. Every word, every letter, every accent of the Veda had been settled by authority as far back as about the fifth century B.C., and from that point of view the authority of oral tradition was, and is still considered much higher than that of a mere manuscript. Formerly, as in the time of the Laws of Manu, it was even forbidden to write the Veda or to sell copies of it. That so sacred and more than sacred a work should have been published for the first time by a barbarian, and that hundreds of copies of it should suddenly be for sale in the streets of Benares, Bombay, and Poonah, was at first a very great shock to the orthodox. Still, though there were protests, and though all sorts of doubts were thrown on the genuineness of the printed text, even the most bigoted opponents of everything European had at last to give in, and to confess that the printed text was really their true Veda, and that it was more complete and more correct than any manuscript then in existence.

We must never forget that the ancient literature of India was entirely mnemonic. This may sound almost incredible, yet there are few Sanskrit scholars who would any longer doubt it. In their recognised system of education the imprinting of the ancient books on the memory of the young was the most essential feature. Boys, not girls, had to spend years and years of their youth, while staying in the house of a Guru, in learning by heart line after line of certain books, and nothing else. Thus only can we account for the wonderful capacity and tenacity of their memory. They at first learnt their sacred books, as I have known children to learn poems in a foreign language, without even attempting to understand a single word. Children of good Brâhman families were simply treated like sheets of paper, on which the teacher impressed letters, syllables, words, and sentences by sound only. Later only came the time for going over (Adhyayana) what stood thus imprinted on their memory, and for understanding, under the guidance of qualified teachers, its real purport. This, too, may seem almost incredible to us, but in the absence of writing and printing, what else could have been done? Every boy who passed through the orthodox system of education (Brahma*k*aryâ) became a copy of whatever text he was made to learn, and this copy had to be kept in good condition by constant repetition. Unless we keep this clearly before our mind, we shall never understand the state of ancient literature in India, with all its changes and chances, before the introduction of writing. When we consider, for instance, the enormous bulk of the ancient Sanskrit epic, the Mahâbhârata, a poem of more than 90,000 couplets, four volumes quarto, we hesitate before accepting it as a mnemonic poem. And yet we have what amounts to almost positive evidence of the poem having existed before the introduction of writing into India, in the fact that there is an episode, added at the beginning of the poem, in which we are told how the whole poem was reduced to writing by the god Ga*n*e*s*a, and that this episode is absent in many MSS., particularly those of the South of India. And even after the introduction of writing every precaution was taken to keep certain sacred texts from being written down, so as to force each rising generation to learn their literature, sacred and profane, from the mouth of a teacher, and not from a manuscript. Even to the present day this old system of imprinting whole books on the brain has not been allowed to become entirely obsolete, and the mnemonic achievements which in several cases I have witnessed myself in young men when they come to Oxford are almost unbelievable.

A printed edition of their sacred Rig-Veda was therefore, even under the changed circumstances of the nineteenth century, a kind of monstrosity.

Among the first to recognise my edition of the Rig-Veda was the Râjah Râdhâkânta Deva, and his recognition was all the more important to me as he stood at the head of the strictly orthodox and conservative party in Bengal. He himself had no doubt that the whole Veda was really the eternal word of God, and that an unswerving faith in it was the *sine quâ non* of a religious and pious life. Even such highly esteemed books as the Laws of Manu, the Mahâbhârata and the Purâ*n*as had to give way before it, if there should ever be any difference between them and the Veda. We can hardly imagine how people in India could live in such an atmosphere, but it evidently agreed both with those who thought for themselves and with those who thought as they were bid.

My friend, Râdhâkânta, however, made some reservations. The Rig-Veda, he said, though far the most important, is only one out of four Vedas which, though all founded on the Rig-Veda, have each certain portions peculiar to themselves. This no one would have denied, but what are the hymns of all other so-called Vedas put together, if compared with the Rig-Veda ? They are mere sacrificial prayer-books, most of their hymns being taken from the Rig-Veda, and the Atharva-Veda being confessedly a later collection, though it contains curious remnants of Indian popular poetry, incantations, medical formulas, and the like. If all had been lost, except the Rig-Veda, the loss would not have been very great, at least so far as the study of ancient mythology and religion was concerned. Of course I had studied the Yagur-Veda, and had actually copied the whole of it with Mahîdhara's commentary at Paris. This was published afterwards by Professor Weber from my own copy which I had presented to him. I could also tell my Indian friend that we possessed in Germany an edition of the Sâma-Veda by Benfey, and were expecting an edition of the Atharva-Veda by Roth. These were editions of the hymns of the four Vedas, but I could assure him that even the Brâhmanas, on which he laid great stress as being the highest authorities for sacrificial rules, for traditions, and ancient customs, were no longer hidden from us, but ready to be published by scholars such as Haug, Weber, Aufrecht, and others. But even then he would still make his reservations. We might know one *S*âkhâ, or text, he said, of each of their sacred books; but, in conformity with the highest theological authorities, he maintained that there existed formerly many more of such texts which had become extinct; but which nevertheless must be admitted as the original authority for any doctrines or customs not sanctioned by the Vedas, such as we possess them now. The first part of this argument I readily granted, but I had to demur to the second, because anything, even the most degrading customs, might thus have been invested with a divine sanction.

And so it was, as is well known by this time, in the case of Sutti, or the burning of widows, a custom which, though it had long ago been abolished by law, gave rise to a long and animated controversy between the old Râjah, Professor Wilson, and myself.

To show what kind of man the Râjah was, I shall here give some specimens of his letters. It is difficult to do this, because, as I stated before, the style adopted by Hindus in writing letters, whether in Sanskrit or in English, is so flowery and ornate that, particularly when it is addressed to oneself, it seems very conceited and egotistical to publish any of their laudatory remarks. Allowance must be made for Oriental phraseology, and all superlative expressions have to be considerably reduced in English before they reach the level of reality.

In November, 1851, the Râjah, when sending me his Thesaurus, wrote:—

"When I ventured to assume the character of a lexicographer, my most ambitious wish was but to revive the study of Sanskrit in my own country, where it has been on the decline; but I should not dissemble that love of fame stimulated my exertions through worldly tribulations, where patience must have failed and perseverance wearied. I devoted the greatest portion of my life and no inconsiderable amount of labour and expense to the execution of the work; and though as an encyclopædist I have no claim to originality, or to the merits of genius, yet, I trust, my industry and application will, at least, be applauded when I may be considered as a humble pioneer of Sanskrit learning. I have endeavoured to obtain the approbation of those whose good opinion one cannot but be proud of and solicitous to secure; nor is it an inconsiderable reward of my labour that it has deserved the commendation of a Müller and a Wilson, who have won golden opinions by their profound scholarship in Sanskrit."

To be named by the side of Wilson was a compliment highly appreciated by a young man of twenty-eight, as I then was, and I may be pardoned for having felt flattered at the time more than was perhaps quite right, by the old Râjah's well-turned phrases.

Then, turning to my edition of the Rig-Veda, my correspondent continued:—

"I have lately been honoured by the Honourable the Court of Directors with the present of the first volume of your noble and excellent edition of the

Rig-Veda, published under their patronage. Some time ago when I received your specimen copy of it, which you had so politely desired Dr. Roer to send me, I read it with eagerness, and, although I was obliged to return it sooner than I could have wished, I saw enough to convince me that you would go far beyond all expectation, and your present publication has confirmed this opinion.

"Arduous and novel as is the undertaking you have entered on amidst a variety of disadvantages, the able and masterly manner in which you have begun to execute it displays your profound erudition, critical acumen, and unparalleled industry of research; you stand forth a very illustrious example of uncommon ardour and undaunted perseverance, such as is not to be cooled by discouragement, nor obstructed by difficulty; your labours will furnish the Vaidik Pandits with a complete collection of the Holy Sanhitâs of the first Veda, only detached portions of which are to be found in the possession of a few of them, and enable the student of antiquity 'to snatch the veil that hung her face before,' supply materials for the history of the ancient East—nay, ancient world, and rear up for you a monument more durable than brass."

I confess I feel somewhat ashamed of copying this panegyric, but no one will suspect me of having believed a word of it. It seemed to me, however, that a letter so well conceived and so well expressed was worthy of being preserved as showing a phase through which the Indian mind had to pass, and which by this time it has left behind. If we consider how different the trend of native thought really is from our own, we shall have to confess that few, if any, European scholars have ever mastered any Oriental language to the same extent as the writer of this letter has mastered English, or have adapted their thoughts so cleverly to English models as this old Râjah.

Let us see now how he arranged the facts of the case, so as to satisfy his own mind :—

"It is surely," he continues, "a very curious reflection on the vicissitudes of human affairs that the descendants of the divine Rishis (prophets) should be studying on the banks of the Bhâgîrathî (Ganges), the Yamunâ (Jumna), and the Sindhu their Holy Scriptures as published on the banks of the Thames by one whom they regard as a distant Mlechchha, and this Mlechchha, the descendant of the degraded Kshattriyas (noblemen), according to our *S*âstras, and claiming a cognate origin with the Hindus, according to the investigations of the modern philologists, who will ere long rise to the rank of a Veda-Vyâsa (arranger and revealer of the Veda) of the Kaliyuga.

"Though our *S*âstra is deemed the grand and primeval fountain from which the present streams of knowledge that run through the civilised countries of the globe have taken their rise, yet it has not been considered as defiled by receiving into it a foreign tributary. As Yavanâchârya (a Greek teacher) gave to the Hindus his system of astronomy many centuries ago, so the German Bha*tt*a (Doctor) is now giving them his edition of the Rig-Veda, and will, as he promises, furnish them with his commentaries upon them."

If we wish to understand and to appreciate the effort made by this highly educated Indian nobleman, to digest what must have been a hard morsel to his orthodox mind, the edition of his own sacred book by a German or an Englishman, let us try to imagine what it would have been to us if the New Testament, never printed before, had been published for the first time, not by a Dutch scholar, such as Erasmus, but by a Hindu at Benares. We know how great was the commotion when, after the invention of printing, Erasmus published the first critical edition of the New Testament. We must not imagine that the feelings of awe and reverence for their Veda were different from our own for the Bible. To have this book, which few only had ever seen before in India, sent to them from London and offered for sale, proved indeed a great shock to the Hindu conscience, nor was it easy for many of their priests to take the same dispassionate view as this enlightened Râjah. He had by no means broken with his religious convictions or national prejudices, and in his eyes, in spite of all his kindness and politeness, I was and could be no more than a Mle*kkh*a, that is a barbarian. As I had never been in India and could never, like so many other scholars, have availed myself of the valuable assistance of native Pandits, it seemed to him impossible to account for my knowledge of Sanskrit, particularly of the obscure and difficult Vedic Sanskrit, unless he made me a descendant of certain noble or Kshattriya families who, according to the Purâ*n*as, had been exiled from India many centuries ago. And, as if to quiet his own conscience in accepting my edition of his sacred book as undefiled by the foreign hands through which it had passed, he reminded himself that after Alexander's conquests in India certain Greeks or Yavanas, had acted as teachers to the astronomers of India, and had even been accepted as inspired, so long as they taught what was true. All this shows a most interesting crisis through which the Hindu mind had passed in former times, and had to pass once more, a crisis which, though it has not yet finished, is at all events preparing a religious reformation in

India, by assigning to the Veda its true historical position, as the best that the Hindu mind could have produced four thousand years ago, and that to the present day has retained a certain vitality among the true leaders of the people of India.

I have always been a bad correspondent, finding it quite impossible even at that early time to answer all the letters of my many unknown friends. India, from a very early day in my career, has been smothering me with letters, many of them in Sanskrit or in local dialects which I do not even understand. Now it seems that in this case also I waited for some time before acknowledging so interesting a letter as that of the Mahârâjah. However, I find the draft of a letter to him among my papers, and I may as well give an extract from it here :—

The letter which you addressed to me in 1851 on receiving the first volume of my edition of the Rig-Veda reached me so late that I had nearly finished the second volume of my Rig-Veda, and I therefore postponed writing to you, because I wished at the same time to send this my second volume, if only to show you that I meant what I said, and was determined to carry out my undertaking —namely, to publish in time the whole collection of the sacred hymns of your Rishis, together with the commentary composed in the fourteenth century by the learned Sâya*n*â*k*ârya. I have stated in my Preface how much I owe to your valuable Thesaurus, a work which will make your name not only revered by your own countrymen, but respected among all the scholars of Europe. Tathâ *k*a sruti*h*, Yâvad asmi*n* loke purusha*h* pu*n*yena karma*n*â srûyate, tâvad ayam svarge loke vasatîti. And thus says your Scripture: "So long as a man is known in this world by a good work, so long does he dwell in heaven." . . . How happy I should be if I could spend some time at Calcutta or Benares, and discuss with you and your learned Pandits your ancient religion, your sacred writings, your traditions, and the future of religion in India. It was not mere idle curiosity that led me to a study of the Veda, but a wish to know a work which has been for so many centuries the foundation on which millions and millions of human beings have built up their religious convictions. However much we may differ from the old forms of faith and worship, it is our duty, it seems to me, to approach every religion with respect, nay, with reverence. The vital principle, the original source of religion is the same everywhere; it is faith in a Higher Power, and a belief that our moral life should be such as to please Him to whom we owe our being and to whom we feel bound to ascribe the highest perfection which our limited human faculties can conceive. Nor have I been disappointed by the Rig-Veda, though it is different from what I and others expected. There are large portions in it which have hardly any connection with religion at all, but they are interesting all the same as relics of antiquity, such as the song of the gambler, the dialogue between Lopamudrâ and Agastya, between Yama and Yamî, between Purûravas and Urvasî. Other prayers for health and wealth are appropriate in their simplicity to a very primitive state of society. But there are passages which show a truly religious spirit, such as "Ek*am* sad viprâ bahudhâ vadanti"—"The sages speak in many ways of the One that exists"; "Yo deveshu adhi deva eka âsît"—"He who alone is God above gods." Simple moral sentiments also occur in it which deserve to be treasured; such is "Vi ma*k* *kh*rathâya rasanâm ivâga*h*"—"Loose from me sin like a rope"; "Dâmeva vatsâd vi mumugdhy a*m*ho, na hi tvadâre nimishas *k*a nese"—"Loose from me sin like a rope from a calf, for away from Thee I am not master of a twinkling of the eye." Though their number is small in the Sanhitâ, yet there is so much more simplicity and purity in most of these old hymns that I cannot understand how they could ever have been superseded by the Purâ*n*as, works which from a moral, religious, and intellectual point of view do not seem to me worthy to rank as the Bibles of a nation so highly gifted as the inhabitants of Âryâvarta.

If my edition of the Rig-Veda could help towards bringing the people of India back to the study of what their ancient writers unanimously considered as the highest authority of their religion, it would, I think, be an important step forward, not backward, though I hope that the future has even greater things in store for them than a mere return to their ancient form of belief and worship. We must not forget that, like everything else, religions also grow old and can seldom defy four thousand years. The antiquity of a religion which is often appealed to as a proof of its truth, seems to me to tell in the very opposite direction. The older it is, the more likely it is to have become effete in human hands, and unfit for new times, and to require either reformation or entire abolition, to make room for a new and better form of faith.

I know you are bound to consider me as a Mle*kkh*a, but allow me to say that I do not entertain the same exclusive feelings towards you and your countrymen. And remember that one of your Vedic Rishis says that all the castes, the *S*ûdra as well as the Brâhma*n*a, came from Brahman, and participate, therefore, in the same nature and substance, the Divine in man. We believe that all men are equal before God, and with that feeling and in that spirit I remain, with great respect,

Yours sincerely,

F. MAX MÜLLER.

I shall, with the same caution as before, add one more letter, though I know I shall be very much blamed for doing so. The Râjah in expressing his own sentiments, expressed no doubt the sentiments of the society in which he moved, and the crisis through which the conservative and orthodox party passed at that time, unimportant as it may seem to us, was full of vital problems for the future of the religion of the cultivated classes of India. On March 5, 1855, Râdhâkânta Deva wrote:—

I have lately received through the Bengal Government a copy of the second volume of the Rig-Veda, as a present from the Honourable the Court of Directors, and I can ill express the feelings of mingled joy and admiration with which I grasped this most precious gift. Our Pandits are startled out of their wits, and scarcely credit their senses, when they are told that the sacred volume before them has been edited by a distant European scholar who had no opportunities of consulting with a Vaidik Pandit, who had to collect, copy out, and collate various manuscripts of texts and commentaries, mutilated and corrupted, and to refer to the scanty and almost inaccessible sources of information on the subject for the purposes of ascertaining their genuine reading, and then with aching eyes to revise their proof-sheets.

Great is the obligation under which you have laid the learned world. By your successfully embarking on such an arduous undertaking, you have done to the Hindus an inestimable benefit, supplying them with a correct and superb edition of their Holy Scriptures. Accept therefore my most grateful and sincere thanks, which, in common with my countrymen, I owe you, and my special acknowledgments for the very kind and obliging manner in which you have noticed my name and work in the preface to the second volume of the Rig-Veda. At the conclusion of this preface is to be found a truly poetic touch, a noble, frank, and irresistible gush of feeling for the irreparable loss sustained by the literary world and you personally, on the termination of the earthly career of Eugène Burnouf. I wish I could find terms adequate to respond to your sympathy; we cannot be too lavish of eulogies for his merits, or weary of dirges for his loss. In the few letters he has written to me I find a noble trait of humility and simplicity in his character which is the invariable exponent of a great mind.

In 1833 on the occasion of acknowledging the present of the *S*abda-Kalpa-druma he says: "Ce n'est pas à un Européen qui est à peine sur le seuil de cette vaste science de l'Inde, qu'il appartient dc juger une composition de co mérite et d'une telle étendue. Des hommes comme les Colebrooke et les Wilson, qui ont puisé la grande partie de leurs connaissances à la source des entretiens brahmaniques, sont les juges les plus dignes d'un aussi beau travail."

In 1840, when he had the kindness to send me a copy of his fine edition of the Bhâgavata Purâna, he—the first decipherer of the Cuneiform inscriptions—the first Pali scholar and historian of Buddhism—the first editor and interpreter of the Zend-Avesta—and the great Sanskrit philologist—thus speaks of himself: "Mais, vous songerez que c'est l'œuvre d'un lointain Mletchha qui ne fait que commencer à balbutier la langue des grands et vénérables Rishis . . . "

Wishing you a long life to crown all your undertakings with success, and requesting you to offer my best regards to my learned friend Professor Wilson, I remain with great respect,

Yours sincerely,

RÂDHÂKÂNT, RÂJA BAHADOOR.

I repeat once more that I must decline all the undeserved compliments paid to me by my Indian correspondents, who, though they show so perfect a mastery of English, are hardly aware that in the North our language is less warm and less sunny than in the South, and that we leave many things unsaid which must bring a blush to the cheeks of everybody who knows himself, and knows how very imperfect his knowledge really is, and how far below his ideals the execution of the work of his life has remained. If Burnouf said that he was only beginning to stammer Sanskrit, what shall I, his unworthy pupil, say? But the letters themselves are important as showing the attitude assumed by the conservative orthodox party in India, when the first edition of their Sacred Book fell among them like a bombshell. For years, for centuries, nay for thousands of years, this Veda on which their whole religion was founded had been to them a kind of invisible power, much as the Bible was in the early centuries of the Papacy, when the privileged only were supposed to know it and were allowed to interpret it. In discussions between Brâhmans and Christian missionaries, this Veda had always been the last stronghold of the Brâhmans. Whatever was held up to them as a doctrine peculiar to Christianity, was met by them with the ready reply that it had been taught long ago in the Vedas also. But this Veda itself was never produced when they were asked to point out chapter and verse. Long after the manuscripts of other Sanskrit texts had been communicated to English students, the MSS. of the Veda were kept apart, and the touch, nay the very look of an unbeliever, was supposed to desecrate them. And now the book was there, handled by everybody, and spelt out more or less successfully by anybody acquainted with Sanskrit.

The Brâhmans always accept the inevitable, but we shall see how, with a better knowledge of the Veda, there sprang up discussions as to its divine or revealed character, and how these discussions led gradually to the formation of a new religious sect, which, though at present confined to small circles, will no doubt in the end stir the millions, and produce a reformation in a country which seemed to be unchangeable. Of this I shall have to speak later on, when I gather up my reminiscences of Keshub Chunder Sen and his fellow-workers. Movements in which we are interested and engaged ourselves from their beginnings seem generally much smaller to us than they really are in the light of history. When Luther was translating the Bible in the castle of the Wartburg, he little dreamt that he was laying the foundation of a new Church in Germany and in all Teutonic countries, nor did Rammohun Roy on his death-bed at Bristol foresee what would grow up from the few hints he had thrown out as to the possibility of a reform and a revival of the ancient national religion of his country. But Debendranâth followed, Keshub Chunder Sen followed, and if the fire they lit does not at present burn and shine so brightly as it ought, it will certainly not die, but burst out again; for the way which those heroes pointed out is the only possible way leading from the past to the future, from ancient to modern religion, from darkness to light. Many who have lived in India and who imagine that they know India, because they know Calcutta or Bombay, are inclined to shrug their shoulders and to look down with superior wisdom and pity on those misguided dreamers, as they call them, who imagine that they can guide millions to a higher and more truly religious life. We may not live to see the hopes of Rammohun Roy or Keshub Chunder Sen realised; but, as certainly as the sun rises in the morning, the new light for India will break forth from that East to which those prophets and martyrs pointed in the last moments of their life.

The Râjah Râdhâkânta Deva was a conservative of the purest water, not touched as yet even by that conservative liberalism which guided Debendranâth Tagore and made him sympathise with, though it kept him for a time aloof from, his bolder pupil and friend, Keshub Chunder Sen. He himself seems to have never doubted the divine authority of the Veda, and in a curious controversy which I had with him on the Burning of Widows he held his ground firmly as a defender of the old ways. As we became better acquainted with the Veda, it became perfectly clear that the verse from the Rig-Veda which was cited by the Brâhmans as the supreme command for the burning of widows, had been tampered with. The Brâhmans themselves seem to have felt that so barbarous and murderous a custom as the burning of widows, whatever its origin may have been, could only be defended by an authority that was admitted to be infallible and superhuman. Such was the Rig-Veda, and they did not shrink from altering a verse which occurred in a funereal hymn of that Veda, so that instead of conveying a command to the widows to return to their home after having performed the last duty to their departed husbands, it came to mean that they should enter into the womb of fire to follow their husbands to a better world. How such a falsification could have been committed is difficult to understand, when we consider that at first the falsification had to be made in the thousands of memories which represented the real copies of the Rig-Veda. It must have taken place at a very early time, because cases of Sutti do occur, if not in the Rig-Veda, at least in the ancient popular tradition of India, as represented to us in the Mahâbhârata. Even Râdhâkânta Deva seemed inclined at last to agree with me that in the Veda, as we possess it, there is no direct command for this terrible custom ; but he took his stand on the old tradition and maintained that we did not possess the whole of the ancient Vedic literature, and that the authority for the old custom may have existed in one of the lost *S*âkhâs or branches of the Veda. This was a favourite argument with Indian casuists, but Indian casuists had likewise found an answer to it. They called it the "skull argument," and reasoned that as little as a skull could be accepted as a witness in a court of law, could a lost *S*âkhâ of the Veda be appealed to as an authority for a custom like the burning of widows.

All this gives us an insight into the thoughts that rule Indian society, of which even those who spend their best years in India have hardly any suspicion. That an educated Hindu should defend the burning of widows seems strange; still, if Popes and Cardinals could defend auto-da-fés or the burning of heretics, nay, even of witches, because the fire would purify and save their souls which could not be saved otherwise, why should not an Indian Râjah have been convinced that the burning of widows could not be wrong, believing, as he did, that it was enjoined by a lost *S*âkhâ of the Veda, and that the poor women could not be saved unless they followed their husbands on their heels into another world. These are ingrained feelings, and every Hindu would at once recite the popular verses, "Accompanying her husband, she shall reside so long in Svarga

(Heaven) as are the thirty-five millions of hairs on the human body."

A loyal wife is defined as "she whose sympathy feels the pains and joys of her husband, who mourns and pines in his absence, and dies when he dies."

In theory this is all very beautiful, and that there may have been cases where a widow wished to be burnt on her husband's pile, can hardly be doubted.* It is well known that this custom of widow-burning, or of widows dying with their husbands, was by no means confined to India; but it is known also, now that the pages of the Veda are open to us, that the Veda certainly does not countenance it. The custom seems to have arisen with the warrior caste, and I still feel inclined to think that in its origin it was voluntary, and arose from blind, passionate love, and a strong belief in an immediate meeting again in a better world. The idea that its object was to deter wives from poisoning their husbands is simply preposterous, and though it may be quite true that at present the life of a widow has been rendered so miserable that many would willingly prefer death to so wretched an existence as that of a widow, that too could not account for so ancient and so widely spread a custom.

* Chips from a German Workshop, vol. iv., pp. 35-9.

In our own ancient Teutonic mythology, when Baldur had been murdered and his body had been placed in a ship to be carried out to sea, his wife, Nanna, died of grief, and was burnt with him on the same pile.* And Gudrun (Brynhild) also, after Sigurd had been slain, had but one wish, to be burnt with him on the same pile, two servants at their head and two at their feet, two dogs also and two hawks, and the biting sword between them, tho same sword that lay between them when they slept together on the same bed, like brother and sister.† There is humanity in all that inhuman barbarism, if only we try to discover it. The strange part is that this human feeling should have manifested itself in the women only, and never in the men.

* Edda, Gylfaginning, 49.

† Sigurdakwida, iii., 64 ; Helreidh Brynhildar, 12.

MY INDIAN FRIENDS

II

NÎLAKA*NTH*A GOREH

IF I knew the Râjah Râdhâkânta Deva by correspondence only, the next son of India whom I came to know, and for a time very intimately, as one knows and loves a friend, had travelled all the way from India, having come to England with Dhulip Singh. While I was sitting in my room at Oxford copying Sanskrit MSS., a gentleman was shown in, dressed in a long black coat, looking different from my usual visitors, and addressing me in a language of which I did not understand a single word. I spoke to him in English, and asked him what language he was speaking, and he replied with great surprise, "Do you not understand Sanskrit?" "No," I said, "I have never heard it spoken, but here are some MSS. of the Veda which will interest you." He was delighted to see them, and began to read, but he had soon to confess that he was not able to translate a single word. When I expressed my surprise—

though perhaps I ought not to have done so—he told me that he did not believe in the Veda any longer, but had become a Christian. His countenance was most intelligent, and almost heavy with thought, his language and his manners most winning, and we were soon deep in conversation. His name had been Nîlaka*nth*a Goreh—Nîlaka*nth*a being a name of *S*iva (the Blue-neck)—but had been changed into Nehemiah Goreh, when he became a Christian. I have tried to find out more about his birthplace and his parents, but in vain; and, after all, who cares for all these monotonous details with which biographers generally fill the first chapters of their books? Nor did I care much for them myself, except to know that he came from a highly respected Brâhman family, and that his father had been an educated man and a Sanskrit scholar. What I really cared for was the man himself, such as he stood before me, a man, I should have guessed, of about five-and-twenty, glowing with youthful enthusiasm, and evidently brimful of thought. I must leave it to others to supply the year of his birth and all the details of his paternal and maternal genealogy.

It was not long before I discovered a sad and perplexed tone in his conversation, and, though he assured me that nothing but a deep conviction of the truth of Christ's teaching had induced him to change his religion, he told me that he was in great anxiety and did not know what to do for the future. What he had seen of England, more particularly of London, was not what he had imagined a Christian country to be. His patron, Dhulip Singh, had placed him at some kind of missionary seminary in London, where he found himself together with a number of what he considered half-educated and narrow-minded young men, candidates for ordination and missionary work. They showed him no sympathy and love, but found fault with everything he did and said. He had been, as I soon found out, a careful student of Hindu philosophy, and his mind had passed through a strict philosophical discipline. Hindu philosophy is in many respects as good a discipline as Plato or Aristotle, and, Christian though he was, he was familiar with the boldest conceptions of the world, as found in the six systems of Hindu philosophy, and he could argue with great subtlety and accuracy on any of the old problems of the human mind. The fact was he stood too high for his companions, and they were evidently unable to understand and appreciate his thoughts. He did not use words at random, and was always ready to give a definition of them, whenever they seemed ambiguous. And yet this man was treated as a kind of nigger by those who ought to have been not only kind, but respectful to him. He was told that smoking was a sin, and that he never could be a true Christian if he abstained from eating meat, particularly beef. He told me that with the greatest effort he had once brought himself to swallow a sandwich containing a slice of meat, but it was to him what eating human flesh would be to us. He could not do it again. When he thus found himself in this thoroughly uncongenial society, and saw nothing in London of what he had supposed a Christian city to be, he ran away, and came to Oxford to find me, having heard of my interest in India, in its religion, and its ancient literature. He had evidently dreamt of a Christian country where everybody loved his neighbour as himself; where everybody, if struck on the right cheek, would turn the other also; where everybody, when robbed of his coat, would give up his cloak also. All this, as we know, is no longer the fashion in the streets of London, and what he actually saw in those streets was so different from his ideals that he said to me, "If what I have seen in London is Christianity, I want to go back to India; if that is Christianity, I am not a Christian." This sounded very ominous, and I hardly knew what to say or what to do with him. He was not a man to be smoothed down by a few kind words. I tried to find out first why he had given up his native religion, and the more I heard, the more I was amazed. He began life as a worshipper of *S*iva, had then chosen K*r*ish*n*a as his deity, and, dissatisfied with this form of worship also, had proceeded to study the Korân. All that time he had kept carefully aloof from Christian missionaries and Christian converts. But when he saw that the Korân also was full of contradictions and of things which he could not approve, he began to study by himself both the Old and the New Testament. Saturated as he was with philosophical ideas, he soon found that these books also did not satisfy his yearnings, and he wrote, as I was told, two essays in Sanskrit, one against the Old, the other against the New Testament, both directed against a book written by my old friend, J. Muir, the Mataparîkshâ (Examination of Doctrines). Those who knew him at the time in India say that his answer to the Scotch scholar was in flowing and melodious Sanskrit, and was "alike most classical in diction and irrefragable in reasoning." Christianity in India, even as represented by so enlightened a Christian as J. Muir, was supposed to have received its death-blow by it. But the fact was, that in studying the New Testament and trying to refute it, he had become a Christian unawares.

When I asked him to tell me how in the end he

succumbed, and was satisfied with the religion of Christ, he shook his head and said, "I can explain everything, I can explain why I rejected *S*iva, and K*r*ish*n*a, and Allah, and tell you everything that kept me back so long from Christianity, as preached to us in India, and made me reject the New as well as the Old Testament as unsatisfactory to a thinking man. But why and how I became a Christian I cannot explain. I was caught as in a net, and I could not get away from Christ." This did not quite satisfy me, and I pressed him hard several times to find out whether there had not been any other inducement, perhaps unknown to himself at the time, that might have influenced him in taking this momentous step. But it was all in vain. So far from there being any worldly motives mixed up with his conversion, all outward circumstances, on the contrary, were strongly against his professing himself a Christian. He could not tell me of any missionary or teacher whose personal influence might directly or indirectly have told on him.

No one was more surprised than the clergyman to whom he wrote that he was a Christian; that he required no instruction or persuasion, but simply wished to be baptized. His mind was like a crystal, perfectly bright and transparent. He held nothing back from me, but the answer which I most cared for, he could not give. His father, a learned man, holding a high place among the Brâhmans socially, a kind of bishop or dean, as we should call it, owed it to his position, not only to disown, but to disinherit, nay, publicly to curse, his son. The loss of his fortune was nothing to the son; but when it came to the curse, the father himself shrank back. He loved his son, and it is hinted that to a certain extent he may have shared his feelings. So, in order to evade the necessity of the curse, he retired from the world and took upon himself the vow of perpetual silence (Mauna-vrata). We wonder at the Trappists and their silence, but they at all events live in company with other Trappists. But to be silent among friends who speak must be a greater trial still. These men generally retire from the world altogether. Nehemiah Goreh's father, after he had retired into the forest, never uttered a single word again to any human being. He disappeared altogether, and, though for several years his son and his friends hoped that he would return, he never came back. He probably went out of his mind, and died, as many Sannyâsins die in the forests of India. There are more tragedies in heaven and earth than are dreamt of in our philosophy. Nor was that all. Even his wife was taken away from the new convert, though she really was devoted to her husband. Timid as Hindu ladies are, his young wife had been frightened when asked before a judge whether she would remain with her apostate husband or return to her parents. This is what the law enjoins in case of a husband becoming a Christian. But after she had taken refuge in her parental home she repented, and wished to join her husband again. And here a curious scene occurred. The husband actually had to elope with his own wife, and carry her off by main force. After that the law allows a new appeal; the guilty couple were brought once more before a judge, and when the young wife (she was only thirteen) was asked once more what she wished to do, she declared publicly that she would return to her husband, and was then allowed to return to her forsaken home. What more could a man sacrifice for his religious convictions? All I can say is that in the whole of my life I have never seen so true a Christian, so true a martyr, as Nehemiah Goreh. Few Christians, not even bishops, would have passed through such ordeals unscathed. And with all that, he was a philosopher, he knew what philosophy could say and had said on the possibility of revelation and of religion, and yet he was perfectly satisfied with Christianity in its very simplest form. One thing he said sometimes, to account to me for the momentous step he had taken, and for the sacrifices he had made to retain his inward honesty. "Christianity is so pure," he said. One can quite understand how this purity must have told on a mind that had waded through the impurities of the sombre worship of *S*iva, and the lascivious innuendos of the legends of K*r*ish*n*a and the shepherdesses, however much they may be explained as a mere allegory. Even as an allegory the story of a god who carries off the clothes of the shepherdesses while bathing, is not edifying. If it is meant for devotion without guise or disguise, the meaning is too much hidden for ordinary mortals. We may be able to account historically or mythologically for many excrescences of religion, but we cannot dispute them away, nor can we wonder that a pure mind, sickened by them, should turn with a delightful relief to the pure and fresh atmosphere of Christianity.

There was for a time real danger of Nehemiah's falling into utter despair, and all that his friends could do was to send him back, as soon as possible, to India, and to find him some occupation there as a teacher and Scripture reader. There, what seems almost an innate tendency of the Indian mind soon developed itself in Nehemiah, namely, asceticism and a complete renunciation of the world. For a time he was attracted by outward ceremonial and symbolism, and found comfort in it; but when that also failed to satisfy him, he became, to all intents and purposes, a Christian Sannyâsin (hermit). For himself he wanted nothing, even controversy had no longer any charm for him; though, in the essays which he was induced to address to his countrymen on the insufficiency of the six systems of native philosophy, he proved himself a subtle critic of Hinduism, and a powerful defender of Christianity. These essays, originally written in Hindi, have been translated into English by Dr. Fitz-Edward Hall, under the title of "Rational Refutation of the Hindu Philosophical Systems," Calcutta, 1862, and they are extremely interesting and useful.

Judging from letters which I received from him from time to time, he never quite recovered the balance of his mind. His trials had been too much for him. Not only had he lost his father and his wife, but he became separated even from his children, so that no cares of this world should disturb his peace with God and in God. But to give up a religion—the religion of our father and mother, the religion of our childhood and of all our friends, however imperfect it may be from our own point of view, inflicts a wound that heals but slowly, and is apt to break open again and again. Why should missionaries fail to see this, and expect from their heathen pupils sacrifices which they themselves would shrink from by a natural instinct of self-preservation? It is no answer to say that the religion of those whom they wish to bring over to Christianity is antiquated, vulgar, hideous, and false. The religion in which a man is born, the religion of a man's father and mother, has always something sacred in it that ought to be respected. Is there a single missionary who, if he had been born a Hindu or a Parsi, would have embraced Christianity without a struggle? When we consider how unimportant the differences are between the religion of reformed and unreformed Christians if compared with the treasures that both share in common, why should it be such a wrench for a Roman Catholic to become a Protestant, except that his father and mother were Roman Catholics? The points of difference between them are all, without exception, the work of men, and often of men who have no very high record in the pages of history. Yet to give up the mass for the eucharist, the wafer for the bread, the mixed for the pure wine, has often been too much even for a truly Christian heart, and has separated those who were meant to be brothers in Christ. I say all this only in order to make people understand what trials and tortures Nehemiah Goreh had to undergo before he could take that step which, from a missionary point of view, seems so easy and natural. To be torn away from all our friends, to think that they are all wrong and we alone are right, was too great an effort to a sensitive mind, such as his was, and left a wound behind which it required a very strong and healthy nature to bear and many years to heal. That he should have become a kind of Christian Sannyâsin, or anchorite, was natural; that he should have been attracted for a time by childish ritualism was a pity. This, however, was chiefly due to personal influences, and, if it in any way soothed his broken spirits, no one would grudge him such anodynes. I was much touched when, in one of his later letters, after expressing his perfect satisfaction with what Christianity had given him, he added, "Yet, I often feel like a man who has taken poison." He was for many years a useful member of a Christian brotherhood at Sigra, founded by the Rev. R. M. Benson, whom I remember meeting often in old days in the cheerful common-room of Christ Church. They were very kind to him, and he was most grateful to his brothers. Yet I feel doubtful whether even they understood him fully, and made allowance for all his troubles and all his sacrifices.

When Nehemiah Goreh was in England for the last time, and staying at Oxford, he was not allowed to come to see me, except on the very day of his departure. This was unkind to both of us; he was in no more danger from me than I was from him. I know that in his early days he had used the wings of his mind with great freedom, that he had tried to soar to the highest abodes of the divine, and to fathom the deepest abysses of human nature, fearless of all consequences. He reminded me in that respect of Dr. Pusey, who often declared that he had studied more heresy than anybody else; but, having seen the horrors of utter darkness on every side, he felt it his duty to warn others, and to keep them from seeing what he had seen. Strange only that Nehemiah, brought up as he had been in the doctrines of the Vedânta, should not have seen how even the highest heights and the deepest depths which can be reached by the human mind are lighted up by the omnipresence of Brahman, the Indian name and concept of what we mean by the omnipresent Father, or, if you like, of that ineffable Godhead of which even the Father is one person only. He had become tired of his lifelong search, and had long closed his eyes to this world of seeming. When at last his heart ceased to beat, he felt satisfied that all was well, and that he was safe in trusting in Christ.

It is curious that he should not have drawn more of his countrymen to follow him. His original conception of Christ's teaching was such that many an excellent Hindu could honestly have accepted it. If anywhere, the harvest is ripe in India, and the labourers are many. Unfortunately his philosophical Christianity became more and more ecclesiastical, nay ritualistic in time, through influences which he was too weak to resist. He might have done a great work in India; but what India wants is the young and vigorous Christianity of the first century, not the effete Christianity of the fifteenth century, still less its poor modern imitations. Much the same opinion was expressed by an Indian correspondent, Mr. Brojolall Chuckerbutty, a personal friend and admirer of Nehemiah Goreh. In one of his letters to me he said: "Years ago I had a long discussion in my own house with Nehemiah Nîlaka*nth*a Goreh concerning the Christian religion. He, of course, tried hard to convert me to his faith. But we arrived at a conclusion in which nothing was concluded. I really could not understand how a man of Mr. Goreh's intelligence and learning, who had discarded Hinduism, could accept, in its stead, popular Christianity which stands on the same level with popular Hinduism. By popular Christianity I mean the Christianity of the Church, as contra-distinguished from the Christianity of Christ."

His friends have sometimes found fault with Nehemiah Goreh for having during the latter part of his life so completely withdrawn himself from the world and its social obligations. But here too we must learn to make allowances for the old Indian leaven. He longed for rest. It was a recognised thing in India—I speak, of course, of ancient India—that a man who had fought his fight might retire from the world, shake off all shackles, and become free, even here on earth. Many left their homes and lived in forests—a most delightful way of life in India. These anchorites, fugitives from the world, wanted very little to support life, and that little, so far as we know, was either supplied by nature or given them readily by the members of their family, or even by strangers. There was no lack of family affection in India, but higher than all worldly affections stood the ideal of Vairâgya, freedom from all desires and passions, freedom from all worldly attachments, freedom from all that must perish, real happiness in the Eternal, in the Self, that is, in God who changes not. Some of the most beautiful poetry of ancient and modern India was inspired by that sentiment of unworldliness, the very opposite of that passionate love and attachment which forms the constant theme of European poetry. Love, so far as it means passion and desire, or exclusive attachment to one person, was considered as of this world, and everything belonging to this world was perishable, and therefore not worthy of our highest affection. The Buddhists adopted the same doctrine, but, while condemning love, they preached pity—a splendid substitute. Father and mother, wife, husband, and children were not excepted. They, too, should never be passionately loved or idolised, but they should always be pitied. That pity means a great deal, it may mean all that is best in love. The very relation in which husband and wife, father and mother, parents and children stood to each other could be of this life only, not of that life in which they neither marry nor are given in marriage, the life that underlies even this life on earth. We find it difficult to enter into these ideas, they are so entirely absent from our own literature, particularly from our poetry; which deals mostly with passionate love, but they were quite familiar to the Hindus. We call them strange and curious and extravagant, and then we have done with them. But the subject is not so easily disposed of, and in a country such as India, it is difficult to say who has chosen the good part. There the man at rest with himself and with his God, the man free from all worldly fetters, was a recognised character, and was allowed to live up to his ideals without let or hindrance. How those ideals were realised we may learn from Indian poetry, from the Vairâgya-*S*ataka, for instance (the century of dispassionateness) ascribed to Bhart*ri*-

hari, and from many similar works. There we read * :—

A hermit's forest cell, and fellowship with deer,
A harmless meal of fruit, stone beds beside the stream,
Are helps to those who long for *S*iva's guidance here,
But be the mind devout, our homes will forests seem.†

A more literal translation would be:

"Dwelling in a hallowed forest, nay fellowship with deer, pure diet of fruit, and stones for beds from day to day, such are the requirements of those who desire to worship Hara; but for those whose minds are entirely fixed and pacified, forest or house is alike." (No. 33, ed. Gopinâth.)

I give a few more verses in prose translations, as more faithful, though less perfect than poetry :—

"The earth has been dug by me in hope of treasure, the ore of the mountains has been melted, the ocean has been crossed, and princes have been zealously served, nights have been passed among the graves with a mind bent on propitiating by charms; yet have I not obtained

* Metrical translation by C. H. Tawney, *Indian Antiquary*, November, 1876.

† That is, if only our mind is quieted, we shall enjoy peace in our own home as well as in a forest. *S*iva is here looked upon as the symbol of the Supreme Spirit.

a doit. O Desire, leave me now!" (No. 4, ed. Gopinâth.)

"Even if they have longer remained with us, the objects of sense are sure to vanish. What difference is there in the separation, that man should not forsake them himself! If they pass away by themselves, they cause the greatest pain to the mind, but if we forsake them ourselves, they cause endless happiness and peace." (No. 16, ed. Gopinâth.)

"When pride is failing, when our wealth has departed, when the beggar has gone away disappointed, when our kinsmen have vanished and our friends have disappeared, and youth is slowly waning, one thing only befits the wise man—to dwell somewhere in the arbour of a cave in the valley of a high mountain where the rocks are sanctified by the milk (waters) of the daughter of *G*ahnu (Gangâ)." (No. 31.)

"In health there is fear of disease, in family-pride fear of a fall, in wealth fear of the king, in silence fear of disregard, in strength fear of an enemy, in beauty fear of old age, in knowledge fear of blame, in virtue fear of calumny, in life fear of death; everything on earth is surrounded by fear; freedom from desires alone gives us freedom from fear." (No. 116.)

"Where before there were many in the house,

there is left only one; where there was one, there are now many, and in the end there is not left even one; thus does Kâla (time), shaking the day and the night like two dice, play cleverly, together with Kâlî (death), with mortals as with figures on a board." (No. 38.)

"Delights are unsteady like lightning, flashing from the midst of a veil of clouds, life is fleeting like a shower from a mass of clouds that have been torn asunder by the wind; the caresses of youth enjoyed by man are fickle. O ye wise, when you have pondered this, set your heart quickly on Yoga that can be gained by perfection of meditation and firmness." (No. 53.)

"You are I, and I am you, such was formerly our mind; what has happened now that you are you and I am I?" (No. 63.)

"What good is there in the Vedas, the Smṛitis, the reciting of the Purâṇas, and all the tedious Śâstras, or in the trouble of performing sacrifices which are to reward us with an abode in the arbours of the gardens of Svarga? If we except only the compassing of an entrance into that place where there is bliss in oneself and which is like the fire at the end of the world which destroys all that produces pains by means of the fetters of existence, everything else is a mere matter of bargain." (No. 79.)

"O mother Earth, father Wind, friend Light, kinsman Water, brother Sky, I fold my hands in adoration to you. I, with whom the burden of all ignorance has been cast off by means of bright and spotless knowledge; I, shining with increase of good works produced through contact with you, I now melt away in the Highest Spirit (Brahman)." (No. 85.)

Ideas like these, very beautiful when clothed in the beautiful language of ancient India, seemed never to be absent from the mind of my friend, though modified by the Christian atmosphere in which he had learnt to breathe. He too would have been happiest in the forest, on the banks of the Ganges—a stone for his couch, the deer for his friends, wild fruits for his food, lost in his God, who was more to him than a mere Jehovah, more also than the Brahman of the multitude. He might have called him Brahman, hidden under the features, or under the *pratîka* (*persona*) of a father. He himself, however, had soared higher and discovered the true Brahman in himself, and with all these exalted ideas he had found rest and happiness in the humble faith of a Christian. With him Christianity would have been perfectly compatible with Indian philosophy, particularly the Vedânta, if only properly understood. Men such as Dr. Henry Brown were Christian Platonists at Cambridge; why then should there be no Christian Vedântists, such as Nehemiah Goreh was in the beginning of his career? Later in life the bold eagle became tired, his pinions faltered, and he yearned for his nest. He is at rest now from all his doubts and earthly troubles. His name is known to few only, and will soon be forgotten altogether, like the names of many who were martyrs to their convictions on earth. He had the true courage of his convictions, and in my memory he will always retain his place very near to Stanley, Colenso, and a few others who shall remain unnamed. If he changed later in life, I feel sure that he changed honestly, and that he was as true in his ecstatic adorations (Upâsanâ) as he had been in his philosophy (*Gñâna*).

KESHUB CHUNDER SEN.

While through Râdhâkânta I came in contact with the rigid conservative elements of Indian society, and in Nehemiah Goreh was able to witness the first real conquest achieved by Christianity and its concomitant powers over the Indian mind in its highest excellence—for I doubt whether, if left to itself, the Indian mind could reach a higher degree of intellectual vigour than it did in Nehemiah Goreh—a new phase of Indian life was opened to me through my long friendship with Keshub Chunder Sen. That contact with Christianity would sooner or later produce a fermentation in the religion of India might easily have been foreseen. It was the same when Mohammedanism reached India. Both Mohammedanism and Christianity were modern religions compared with Brahmanism, they belonged to a more advanced state of thought and culture, and were free from many of the childish ideas almost inseparable from an earlier stage of religion in the history of mankind. But, strange to say, the very antiquity of the Vedic religion was looked upon as an argument in its favour, and it certainly made its surrender more difficult to its followers. Nânak, Kabir, Chaitanya, and other reformers, near contemporaries of our own reformers, tried to effect a compromise between the two religions by eliminating the glaring imperfections of the ancient national faith of India, such as idol worship, animal sacrifices, &c., but retaining its sublime moral and philosophical spirit, which, in some respects, was purer and higher than even the doctrines of the Korân. It may be useful to glance at some of these reformers, if only to show that Keshub Chunder Sen was not without his predecessors.

CHAITANYA.

The most important among these reformers about the beginning of the sixteenth century was Chaitanya (1485–1527). At all events he had the largest following and has so even to the present day. He did not perhaps go quite so far as Keshub Chunder Sen, but in many cases this modern reformer seems certainly to have been influenced by the spirit of Chaitanya, nay, in some cases, to have used almost the same words. The followers of Chaitanya, whether they are called Gosains, Bhâgavatas, Vairâgis, or other names, are said to form even now one-fifth of the whole population of Bengal. Whether for rules of life or for doctrine they still appeal to Chaitanya and to his two fellow-workers, Advaitânanda and Nityânanda, as their highest authorities. They are outwardly worshippers of Vishnu in his form of K*r*ish*n*a, but by the more enlightened among them, K*r*ish*n*a or Vish*n*u is conceived as Brahman or the Supreme Spirit. The social importance of this reform consisted chiefly in the complete ignoring of caste. "The teacher of the four Vedas," Chaitanya used to say, "is not my disciple, but the faithful Ka*n*d*â*la (outcast) enjoys my friendship." Even Mohammedans were received as brothers in the faith, in fact the union of Hinduism and Islam was one of the leading ideas of the time. Every true disciple of Chaitanya had the right of begging for alms, and was expected to lead an ascetic life. At the same time there is a verse quoted as coming from Chaitanya, which leaves the impression that his ideas of asceticism were not very strict. "Let all enjoy fish, broth, and women's charms, be happy and call upon Hari (Vish*n*u)." But if he saw no harm in the enjoyment of life, resembling in this another honest reformer, Luther, he protested and warned his disciples against all worldly pleasures that would draw away their thoughts from K*ri*sh*n*a. According to an article lately published in the "Journal of the Buddhist Text Society," 1897, vol. v., Part 4, p. 87, Chaitanya taught, and his followers continue to teach that the original cause of all things was Wisdom. That Divine Soul was believed to vivify all, and to be the Lord of all and the Protector of all. He is called spiritual, pure, and full of ecstacy. The Vedas chant His praises unceasingly. It is this Being, he taught, whom we call K*ri*sh*n*a. This Supreme Being has three phases: (1) Brahman, the light of the world that gives vitality to all. The sages try to reach Him by wisdom. (2) Paramâtman, he who is sentient, omnipresent, and omniscient. The sages go to Him through contemplation or Yoga; and (3) Bhagavat or the Personal God, who manifests Himself in the material world. Men try to reach Him through Bhakti (devotion).

Some ascribe creation to matter: but this, according to Chaitanya, is impossible. What power has inert matter, he asks, that can produce so grand a creation, filled with wisdom and beauty? It is the will of an Almighty Being that brought this universe into existence. It is impossible for man even to think of His greatness.

The human soul, the *G*îvâtman, is, according to Chaitanya, an infinitesimal portion, like a ray, of the Divine Being. God is like a blazing fire, and the souls are like sparks that come out of it. Deluded by Mâyâ, i. e. the attractions of the world, the *G*îvâtman forgets its own nature : but when it has recognised the transitory nature of all things, it goes up again to its Maker.

Many ascribe to this *G*îvâtman the attributes of God. But this, according to Chaitanya, cannot be, because it has an individual character. *S*ruti (revelation) says that he who thinks that he has found out the nature of God knows nothing of Him.

Chaitanya says that it is the duty of every man to adore K*ri*sh*n*a and to perform good deeds without any expectation of rewards. Bhakti (devotion) is the channel that carries man to K*ri*sh*n*a. When a devotee says, "Oh Lord, I am yours," it is then only that he can attain K*ri*sh*n*a.

Lastly, it must be the aim of every man to gain K*ri*sh*n*a's love, and Bhakti is the way that leads to it. Chaitanya defined Bhakti as an uninterrupted tendency of the heart towards God, just like the flow of a river towards the sea.

It is difficult to understand how the followers of Mohammed could ever have been induced to use the name of K*ri*sh*n*a for that of Allah, but we know that it was so, and the same religious amalgamation between Hinduism and Islam was attempted by Nânak, the contemporary of Chaitanya. The Sîkhs, though much changed in time, are the followers of that reformer.

NÂNAK AND THE SÎKHS.

It is a pity that we possess so little trustworthy information about the original Sîkh reformers. Their sacred book, the Granth, exists, nay, it has even been translated into English by the late Dr. Trumpp. But it turns out now that Dr. Trumpp was by no means a trustworthy translator. The language of the Granth is generally called old Penjâbi, and it was supposed that a scholar who knew modern Penjâbi might easily learn to understand the language as it was four hundred years ago. But that is not the case. The language of the Granth is said to be full of local dialectic varieties and forgotten idioms, so much so that it has been said to be without any grammar at all. That is, of course, impossible, for there is method even in what we might call grammatical madness, and we may hope that such a method may in time be discovered. Mr. Macauliffe, who has spent many years among the Sîkhs, and has with the help of their priests paid much attention to their Granth, has given us some most interesting and beautiful specimens of their poetry which form part of their sacred book. Though Nânak was the chief founder of the new religion of the Sîkhs, that is of the *S*ishyas or disciples, other well-known poets, such as Angada, Râmdâs, Râmânand, Kabîr, Farîd (a Mussulman), and Mira Bir, a queen, are mentioned as his helpers and as contributors to the Granth. Râmânand, a Brâhman, or rather a Sannyâsin who had renounced many of the old ceremonial restrictions, on being asked one day to attend a Hindu religious worship, wrote the following lines:

Whither shall I go? I am happy at home,
My heart will not go with me; it has become a cripple.
One day my heart desired to go;
I ground sandal, took attar of roses and many perfumes,
And was proceeding to worship in the temple of Brahm;
But my spiritual guide showed me God in my heart.
Wherever I go I find only water and stones (for bathing
and worshipping);

But thou, O God, art equally contained in everything.
The Vedas and the Purâ*n*as I have all seen and searched.
Go thou thither, if God be not here (in the heart).
O true Guru, I am a sacrifice unto Thee,
Who hast cut away all my perplexities and doubts.
Râmânand's Lord is the all-pervading God,
The Guru's word has cut away millions of acts (sins).

Another and perhaps the greatest among the disciples of Nânak was Kabîr, i. e. the Great. He was strongly opposed to idol-worship. "If God is a stone," he used to say, "I will worship a mountain." Idol-worship was, of course, the greatest stumbling-block in the way of a reconciliation between Hinduism and Islam. Still the defenders of idol-worship and the iconoclastic Mohammedans managed to come to a certain understanding. They agreed to speak each his own language, but to feel that they meant the same. Why cannot Christians and Hindus do the same, particularly when the best spirits among the Hindus at least, have adopted a language which shows that they are very near the Kingdom of God, nearer, I believe, than thousands who are baptised and call themselves Christians? It is most interesting to watch the compromise made between Hinduism and Islam four hundred years ago and to compare it with the compromise between Hinduism and Christianity that is now so eloquently advocated by the followers of Rammohun Roy and Keshub Chunder Sen.

Kabîr said:

What availeth devotion, what penance, what fasting and worship,
To him in whose heart there is worldly love?
O man, apply thy heart to God:
Thou shalt not obtain Him by artifice.
Put away covetousness and regard for what people say of thee.
Renounce lust, wrath, and pride.
By the religious ceremonies (of the Hindus) conceit is produced,
What if they join and worship a stone (they shall receive salvation).
Saith Kabîr, by serving Him I have obtained the Lord.
By becoming simple in heart I have met my God.

How many wear the bark of trees as clothes! What if men dwell in the forest?
What availeth it, O man, to offer incense to idols and drench thy body with ablutions?
O my soul, I know that thou shalt depart.
O silly one, know God!
Wherever I look I see none but those who are entangled in worldly love.
Men of Divine knowledge and meditation, great preachers, all are engrossed in this world's affairs.
Saith Kabîr, without the name of the One God, this world is blinded by Mammon.

By the favour of the Guru the slave Kabîr loveth God,
O Brethren, the Vedas and Mohammedan books are lies, and free not the mind from anxiety.
If for a moment thou restrain thy mind, God shall appear before thee.
O man, search thy heart daily, that thou mayest not fall into despair.
This world is a magic show which hath no tangibility.
Men read falsehood and are pleased; they quarrel over what they do not understand.
The truth is, the Creator is contained in the Creation. He is not of a blue colour, like K*ri*sh*n*a.

Nânak himself expresses his devotion to the true God in the following words:

Were a mansion of pearls erected and inlaid with gems for me,
Perfumed with musk, fragrant aloe, and sandal, so as to confer delight—
May it not be that on beholding it I should forget Thee and not remember Thy name!
My soul burneth without God.
I have ascertained from my Guru that there is no other shelter than thou, O God.
Were the earth to be studded with diamonds and rubies, and my couch to be similarly adorned,
Were fascinating damsels, whose faces shine with jewels, to shed lustre and diffuse pleasure,
May it not be that on beholding them, I should forget Thee, and not remember Thy name!

The following verses will show what was in the

mind of Nânak and of his followers, and we know from history how well their labours for conciliation between Hindus and Mohammedans succeeded, at least for a time, and how what seems to us impossible at present was fully achieved by them. Rammohun Roy and Keshub Chunder Sen would gladly have joined in the following words of the Granth:

> Some men are Hindus and some Musalmans.
> Among the latter are Rawazis, Imams, and Sufis; know that all men are of the same caste.
> The Creator and the Beneficent are the same; the Provider and the Merciful are the same, there is no difference, let no one suppose so even by mistake.
> Worship the One God, He is the one Divine Guru after all; know that his form is one, and that He is the one light diffused in all.
> The Temple and the Mosque are the same, the Hindu worship and the Musalman prayer are the same; all men are the same; it is through error they appear different.
> Allah and Alekh are the same, the Purâ*n*as and the Kurân are the same; they are all alike, it is the One God who created all.

No wonder then that Rammohun Roy and Keshub Chunder Sen should have been hopeful that their endeavours also might be crowned by the same success as Nânak's, and that their new Church would have included not only the believers in the Vedas and the Kurân, but the believers in the Bible also. They both tried very hard to come to an understanding with the representatives of Christianity in India. It is the same even now. There are men who can speak in the name of the Indian people at large, and whose example would tell on the masses who in every country have to be led by their own men of light and leading. Mozoomdar, the natural successor of Keshub Chunder Sen, would not recede a step from the position which his great predecessors took up with regard to Christianity. The idea that his Samâj was in any sense opposed to Christianity or jealous of it would be scouted by him as it was by Keshub Chunder Sen. "Woe unto me," Keshub wrote, "if ever I harboured in my mind the remotest desire to found a new sect, and thus add to the already accumulated evils of sectarianism! Woe unto us, if I ever conceived the project of setting up a movement against the Church of Christ! Perish these lips if they utter a word of rebellion against Jesus. And let the genial currents of my life-blood be curdled at this very moment, if I glory in the hateful ambition of rising against my master. A new sect! God forbid. We preach not a new sect, but the death of sectarianism and the universal reconciliation of all churches. But the very idea of an eclectic church, it will be contended, is anti-Christian. To mix up Christ with the hundred and one creeds of the world is to destroy and deny Christ. To mix Christ with what? What error, with impurity? No. Mix Chri t with all that is Christian in other creeds. Surely that is not un-Christian, far less anti-Christian. In uniting the East and the West, in uniting Asiatic and European faith and character, the Church of the New Dispensation works faithfully upon the lines laid down by Christ, and only seeks to amalgamate the Western Christ and the Eastern Christ. It is not a treaty of Christ with anti-Christ that is proposed, but the reconciliation of all in Christ. It is not the mixture of purity with impurity, of truth with falsehood, of light with darkness, but the fusion of all types of purity, truth and light in all systems of faith into one integral whole. It is the expurgation of anti-Christian elements from the so-called Christian and heathen creeds of the world, and the amalgamation of the pure Christian residuum left. Such is the pure Christian eclecticism of the Church of the New Dispensation."

Men of the type of Rammohun Roy could not, and did not, shut their eyes to the superiority of Christianity from an ethical point of view. They despised in their heart the idols, as worshipped by the vulgar, they saw through the pretensions of their priests, and had long learnt to doubt the efficacy of their sacrifices. But their social institutions were so intimately interwoven with their religion that it required no small amount of moral courage openly to break with it, and to lose caste, that is, to become estranged from all relations, friends, and acquaintances. But while they clearly perceived that their religion was behind the time, and, as a social institution, could not stand long against Christianity, they were by no means inclined to admit that from a philosophical point of view also it was inferior to Christianity. Then was the time when Christianity might have stepped forth in its strong armour and gained its greatest victories in India. Rammohun Roy and his friends were ready. He himself spoke with the greatest humility of the ancient Hindu religion; nay, in conversations with his English friends, he used language far too deprecatory, as it seems to me, of the religious and philosophical inheritance of India. Then was the time to act, but there were no Christian ambassadors to grasp the hands that were stretched out. Such missionaries as were in India then, wanted unconditional surrender and submission, not union or conciliation. In many cases they were themselves fettered by superstitions which men of the type of Rammohun Roy had long discarded. We keep religion and philosophy in different compartments, while with men such as Rammohun Roy the two were one, and the religion of the Veda led naturally on to the philosophy of the Vedânta, which became in turn the firm foundation of their religion. The Vedânta philosophy was so broad that it could well have served as a common ground for religions so different as Hinduism and Christianity undoubtedly are, both in the form of *Gñâna* (knowledge) and of Bhakti (devotion). Rammohun Roy went so far that, when he was in England, it was doubtful whether he, in his mind a Vedântist, was not in his heart a Christian. He spoke with the highest respect and enthusiasm of Christianity, he carefully studied the New Testament, and he willingly joined in Christian worship. Though after his death the Brâhmanic thread was found on his breast, this does not prove that he would not have been willing to surrender that also, if he had met with a real response from his Christian friends on more important subjects. We shall see that some of his followers surrendered even that outward badge of Brahmanism, but they could not surrender that ineradicable belief in the substantial identity of the eternal element in God and in man. A man like Athanasius might easily have brought them to call this consubstantiality the divine sonship of man, if that expression had been fully explained to the Vedântists. But no one was there, nay, no one seems even now bold enough to speak out, and to separate the vital kernel from the perishable crust of religion. That vital kernel was more clearly seen by Rammohun Roy than by many of the missionaries who came to convert him. In Rammohun Roy's translation of the Upanishads we can clearly see that in his view of the Deity and of the relation between the human and the Divine he had never yielded an inch of his old Hindu convictions, though his practical religion was saturated with Christian sentiments. The same mixture of Christian and Hindu thoughts and Christian sentiments may be seen in nearly all the recent reformers of the ancient Hindu religion. The history of these attempted reforms has been so often written that I need not enter more fully into it, beyond repeating my conviction that great opportunities were lost then for planting Christianity on the old and fertile soil of India.

As to Keshub Chunder Sen he was more of a true Christian than many who call themselves Christians, and who are Christians in the ordinary sense of the word. And he knew it and did not deny it. Only he thought that Christianity should not be confined to a small sect, but should comprehend all religions. As Nânak had declared that what was wanted was a religion in which there were all religions, Keshub Chunder Sen also held that Jesus and Moses, Chaitanya and Buddha, Mohammed and Nânak should all become one before God. His New Dispensation was to embrace and unify all religions, all scriptures and all prophets in God, and India was to be the birth-place of that all-embracing religion, because it was the birthplace of the Vedic and the Buddhist religions, and the meeting-place of Christianity and Islam. In one of the last numbers of the "New Dispensation," the organ of the followers of Keshub Chunder Sen, we read:

Who rules India? What power is that which sways the destinies of India at the present moment? You are mistaken if you think that it is the ability of Lord Lytton in the cabinet or the military genius of Sir Frederic Haines in the field that rules India. It is not politics, it is not diplomacy that has laid a firm hold of the Indian heart. It is not the glittering bayonet nor the fiery cannon of the British army that can make our people loyal. No. None of these can hold India in subjection. Armies never conquered the heart of a nation. Muscular force and prowess never made a man's head and heart bow before a foreign power. No. If you wish to secure the attachment and allegiance of India, it must be through spiritual influence and moral suasion. And such indeed has been the case in India. You cannot deny that your hearts have been touched, conquered and subjugated by a superior power. That power need I tell you—is Christ. It is Christ who rules British India and not the British Government. England has sent out a tremendous moral force in the life and character of that mighty prophet, to conquer and hold this vast empire. None but Jesus ever deserved this bright, this precious diadem, India, and Jesus shall have it.

Is it not time to lay hold of these outstretched hands, and not reject them any longer with a cold *non possumus?*

After Rammohun Roy's death there was a pause, for nothing moves in India without a leader, and, though there were followers of the enlightened Râjah, there was for a time no leader of sufficient strength to inspire enthusiasm and to command respect. What happens generally to religious reformers happened in India also. They all agreed in wishing for reform in general, but when it came to settling special reforms, some of no importance whatever, they soon diverged in different directions.

Those who are acquainted with the Vedas, I mean with the hymns and Brâhma*n*as, find it hard to understand how people of enlightened intellect could have hesitated for years and years before deciding against their revealed character. These hymns are not only old, they are antiquated and effete, they have no right, like extinct megatheria, to creep about in the strata in which we live. We are ready to give them a place of honour in our museums, but we cannot allow ourselves to be swayed by them any longer. This may seem a harsh judgment, especially as coming from one who has devoted the best years of his life to the publication of the Rig-Veda, and who certainly has never regretted having done so, as little as he would regret having been the first to unearth the bones of the oldest of all megatheria, or the ruins of Babylon or Nineveh. I am not unaware that there are sparks of profound truth in some of the Vedic hymns, but they form a small portion only of that large collection, and have been brought into focus in the Upanishads and in the Vedânta-Sûtras. With these neither Rammohun Roy nor Keshub Chunder Sen nor Mozoomdar would be willing to part, but to break with anything called Veda was by no means an easy task, even for men of enlightened minds, nor can there be any doubt that the surrender when it took place at last, involved an enormous sacrifice. All that Keshub himself tells us in one of his Lectures is that there was a terrible strife, the strife of conscience against associations of mind and place; duty against prepossessions; truth against cherished convictions. But conscience triumphed over all; the Vedas were thrown overboard by Babu Debendranâth Tagore; and the Brâhma-Samâj bade farewell to their Bible. This step was particularly painful, because all these struggles had to go on before the eyes of foreign observers. In their controversies with the advocates of Christianity, who claimed all the privileges of a revelation for their own Bible, the invariable answer of men like Rammohun Roy had been for a long time "that the Veda also had for thousands of years been considered as divinely inspired." And who could prove that it was not? Arguments in support of the revealed character of the Veda were quickly at hand, for they had been carefully prepared by the ancient theologians of India. And, if the truth must be told, the ideas which missionaries connected with revelation were mostly not very different from those familiar to the Brâhmans. "What argument is there," the Indian apologists asked, "in support of the revealed character of your New Testament which is not equally applicable to the Vedas?" The Buddhists had already said the same to the Brâhmans, though for the sake of argument only, hundreds of years before. "If your Kapila is inspired," they said, "why not our Buddha?" In the same spirit the Brâhmans now said, "If your Christian revelation is claimed as infallible, why should not the Vedic revelation be the same?" The fact was that on one side, as well as on the other, the idea of revelation had lost its original and true meaning; had become purely mechanical, a mere name to conjure with. But the more revelation had become something miraculous in the eyes of the people of India, the more creditable was it that the members of the Brâhma-Samâj, founded by Rammohun Roy, after becoming better acquainted with their own sacred writings than they ever had been before, should solemnly have declared in the year 1850, that the claim of being divinely inspired could no longer be maintained in favour of the hymns and Brâhma*n*as of the Veda. I know of no other instance in the whole history of religions that equals the honesty and self-denial of the members of the Brâhma-Samâj in their throwing down and levelling the ramparts of their own fortress, and opening the gates wide for any messengers of truth. Their honesty will appear all the more creditable when we remember that they were by no means inclined to discard the Vedas altogether, but only declared that reverence for the Deity prevented them from claiming any longer anything like divine workmanship or penmanship for the whole of it. It is a pity that we know so little of the mental struggles through which men like Keshub Chunder Sen and his friends had to pass before they could bring themselves to let go the chief anchor of their religious faith. But Hindus keep their agonies to themselves. No doubt they lose thereby much of that human sympathy which we feel for others who lay open their inmost hearts before us, while slowly surrendering their old for a new, a purer, and a better faith. It is very rare that we are allowed an insight into the home-life and heart-life of eminent Hindus. The female members of their families, the mothers, wives, and sisters, who with us take often so prominent a place in religious struggles, are excluded from our sight altogether. But we know that in India also their influence as mothers and wives is very great. I have several times heard from my more enlightened friends in India that they would like to come to England, or would like to do this or that, but that they shrink from offending their wives or mothers. Women in India, ignorant as they may be, wield great power in their own homes, and it is a common saying that it is easier to defy H. M.'s Secretary of State than to defy one's own mother-in-law. Though mothers and wives are much less enlightened than their husbands and sons, it is for that very reason that they feel the apostasy of their beloved all the more deeply. It is everywhere a more severe trial for a woman than for a man to lose caste, and to lose caste means more in India than it does with us. When now and then we catch a glimpse of what is going on in the sanctuary of an Indian home, we learn that human nature is the same everywhere. Thus we read of the old mother of Keshub Chunder Sen, who must have felt her son's discarding of his old religion very keenly, standing by his deathbed and lamenting that she, poor sinner, should be left behind, while the dearest jewel of her heart was being plucked away from her! And the dying one answers, "Don't say so, dear mother. All that is good in me I have inherited from you; all that I call my own is yours." So saying, he took the dust of her feet and put it upon his head.

When Keshub Chunder Sen arrived in England, he was received with open arms, particularly by the Unitarians. Wherever he spoke or preached, he attracted immense audiences, and his command of the English language, nay his real eloquence produced a deep impression on the religious public in London and elsewhere. I regretted that there was no opportunity of his addressing the young men when he came to Oxford. I was very anxious also that Dr. Pusey should see him, and the kind-hearted old Doctor, friendly as he always was to me, was willing to receive him and to hear what he had to say. Though Dr. Pusey was a scholar, and, as such, above many of the prejudices of his followers, he was not particularly pleased with the speeches made by Keshub Chunder Sen, nor was his close relation with the Unitarians to his theological taste. Still he received him with friendly sympathy, and some very serious questions of religion were discussed by the two men with great freedom. I never kept memoranda even of such important meetings and discussions at which I happened to be present. I thought they would remain engraved on my memory. But now, after the lapse of so many years, I find that it is not so. I have indeed the general impression remaining in my mind, but I cannot trust myself to repeat the actual words that passed, and it would not be fair to give what one thinks was said by such men as Dr. Pusey and Keshub Chunder Sen, when brought face to face, as if it were what was actually said by them. In conversation I have often repeated what passed between them, and this very repetition is apt to mislead a poor memory like my own. I know I cannot trust it as to minute details. I remember, however, very distinctly, how at the end of their conversation, the question turned up, whether those who were born and bred as members of a non-Christian religion could be saved. Keshub Chunder Sen and myself pleaded for it, Dr. Pusey held his ground against us. Much of course depended on what was meant by salvation, and Keshub defined it as an uninterrupted union with God. "My thoughts," he said, "are never away from God;"

and he added, "my life is a constant prayer, and there are but few moments in the day when I am not praying to God." This, uttered with great warmth and sincerity, softened Dr. Pusey's heart. "Then you are all right," he said, and they parted as friends, both deeply moved.

I must say for Dr. Pusey, much as I differed from his views, and much as I regretted some of the steps he took at Oxford, where his influence for a time was very great, he always tolerated me, and befriended me on different occasions. We had a common ground as scholars, and whenever I seemed to go too far for him, I well remember his looking up to the clouds and saying, "Oh, I see you are a German still." When my friends first proposed to the Delegates of the University Press at Oxford my plan of publishing, at Vienna or at Oxford, translations of all the Sacred Books of the East, Dr. Pusey, being a Delegate and a very influential Delegate, strongly supported my plan, only stipulating that the Old and New Testaments should not be included. In vain did I explain to him that these two books could never have a better setting than in the frame formed by the other Sacred Books, and my firm conviction that the time would come when the gap thus left would be greatly regretted; but he remained unshaken. I had to give up a wish that was very near to my heart in order to save the rest, but I still hope that hereafter these two, the most important of the Sacred Books of the East, will find their proper place in my collection. Nothing will serve better to show the difference between these and the rest of the Sacred Books, and to make us see both what they share in common with the rest, and what it is that has given to them the overwhelming influence which they have exercised on the highest destinies of the human race.

When Keshub Chunder Sen was staying with me at Oxford, I had a good opportunity of watching him. I always found him perfectly tranquil, even when most in earnest, and all his opinions were clear and settled. He never claimed any merit for the sacrifices he had made, he rather smiled at what was past, and seldom complained of his opponents, except when they accused him of having been a traitor to his own cause by allowing his daughter to be betrothed and married to the Mahârâjah of Kuch Behar, before she had reached, by a few months, the marriageable age which he and his friends had themselves fixed for all members of the Brâhma-Samâj. This is too long and too complicated a story to be told here; but, whether the father had shown any paternal weakness or not, there was surely no cause for his former friends to separate from him on so paltry aground, to insult him and to break his heart, and in the end to produce a fatal schism in the Brâhma-Samâj. When Keshub Chunder Sen introduced new reforms, surrendering the Vedas, abandoning the Brahmanic thread, sanctioning widow marriages, and forbidding child marriages, his society, hitherto called the Brâhma-Samâj, assumed the new name of the Brâhma-Samâj of India (1861), while the more conservative Brâhmas * under Debendranâth Tagore, were distinguished by the name of Âdi Brâhma-Samâj, or the first Brâhma-Samâj. Those who later on separated again from Keshub Chunder Sen, because they disapproved of the marriage of his daughter, and objected to his claiming, or seeming to claim for himself the gift of inspiration and a higher authority

* Brâhma is the same as Brâhmo; the former Sanskrit, the latter Bengali. Thus, Debendranâth called his book on the Upanishads "Brâhma-dharma*h*," though Brâhma also is a faulty name in Sanskrit.

Samâjes existing in India.

1. Brâhma-Samâj,
Rammohun Roy.

2. Âdi Brâhma-Samâj,
Debendranâth Tagore.

3. Brâhma-Samâj of India,
Keshub Chunder Sen.

4. Sadhâra*n*a Brâhma-Samâj,
Schismatic.

5. Ârya Samâj,
Dayânanda Sarasvati.

than was right for any human being, assumed the new name of Sadhârana Brâhma-Samâj or the Catholic Society of Brâhmas. These different sections carry on the same work, each in its own way. Some see in these divisions signs of healthy vitality, others regret them, as impeding the more rapid advance of a powerful army. The points of difference are so few and so insignificant that it only requires a strong arm to weld them together once more. Protâp Chunder Mozoomdar seemed pointed out for this, and it is to be hoped that he may still succeed in the great work of conciliation.

Many of those who bore the burden of the day, and without whose ready help Keshub Chunder Sen would hardly have been able to achieve what he did achieve in his short life, are by this time dead and forgotten. Even Debendranâth Tagore's constant help and patronage are seldom recognised as they deserve to be in the history of the Brâhma-Samâj. The memory of Hurrish Chunder Mookerjee has lately been revived by the republication of his Three Lectures on Religious Subjects (Calcutta, 1887); and it was his recent death (August, 1898) that reminded the friends of India of the sacrifices made by Râmtonoo Lahari and others in support of the reforms initiated by Rammohun Roy.

RÂMTONOO LAHARI.

Râmtonoo * was born in 1813, and must therefore have been older than Debendranâth Tagore, who is generally considered as the Nestor of the Brâhma-Samâj.

He was a pupil of David Hare, who had undertaken the philanthropic work of educating native youths, and after spending a few years at his school, he was admitted into the Hindu College at Calcutta, which was established in 1817 as the first fruit of the annual vote of £10,000 for educational purposes insisted on by the English Parliament. The teacher who chiefly influenced the young men was D. Rozario, who, though branded by the clergy as an infidel and as a devil of the Thomas Paine school, was worshipped by his pupils as an incarnation of goodness and kindness. It was Christian morality, as preached by D. Rozario, that appealed most strongly to the heart of Râmtonoo and his fellow pupils, many of them very distinguished in later life, the fathers and grandfathers of the present generation of Indian reformers. Râmtonoo became a model among his friends in all matters pertaining to morality and

* Râmtonoo is probably meant for Râmatanu, body of Râma, but when a name has once become familiar in its modern Bengali form, I do not always like to put it back into its classical Sanskrit form.

conscience, penitence and sincerity being the watchwords of his early career, vice and hypocrisy the constant objects of his denunciation, both among his equals and among those of higher rank and authority. Even the founder of the Brâhma-Samâj did not escape his reproof, on account of what he considered want of moral courage to act up to his convictions. As to himself, he denounced caste as a great social and moral evil, and silent submission to superstitious customs as reprehensible weakness. In order to shame those who denounced beef-eating as sinful, he and his friends would actually parade the streets with beef in their hands, inviting the people to take it and eat it. The Brâhmanical thread which was retained by the members of the Brâhma-Samâj as late as 1861, was openly discarded by him as early as 1851. And we must remember that in those days such open apostasy was almost a question of life or death, and that Rammohun Roy was in danger of assassination in the very streets of Calcutta. It is true that European officials respected and supported Râmtonoo, but among his own countrymen he was despised and shunned. However, he continued his career undisturbed by friend or foe, and guided by his own conscience only. Poor as he was, he desired no more than to earn a small pittance as a teacher in public and private schools. Later in life he was attracted to the new Brâhma-Samâj, and became a close friend of Keshub Chunder Sen. When he saw others who spent much time in prayer he considered them as the most favoured of mortals, for pure and conscientious as he was, he felt himself so sinful that he could but seldom utter a word or two in the spirit of what he considered true prayer before the eyes of the Lord. While cultivating his little garden he was found lost in devotion at the sight of a full-blown rose, and while singing a hymn in adoration of God, his whole countenance seemed to beam with a heavenly light. One of his friends tells us that one morning early he rushed into his room like a madman and dragged him out of bed, saying that when the whole nature was ablaze with the light and fire of God's glory, it was a shame to lie in bed. He took the sleeper to the next field, and pointing his finger to the rising sun and the beautiful trees and foliage, he recited with the greatest rapture—what? Not a hymn of the Veda, but some verses from Wordsworth. When his end approached, his old friend Debendranâth Tagore went to take leave of him, and when he left him, he cried: "Now the gates of heaven are open to you, and the gods are waiting with their outstretched arms to receive you to the glorious region." Did the old Vedântist really say "the gods"? I doubt it, unless he used the language of Mâyâ, as we also do sometimes, knowing that his friend would interpret it in the right sense. I see, however, that Mozoomdar also speaks of his spirit reposing in his God—showing how the old habits of thought and old words cling to us and never lose their meaning altogether.

Many more names might be mentioned, but to us they would hardly be more than names. Debendranâth Tagore is the only one left who could give us a history of that important religious movement in India, and of the principal actors in it. But he is too old now to undertake such a task. The others, to use the language of their friends, have, like the stars that rise in the Eastern sky, after completing their appointed journey, sunk below the visible horizon of death, to pass from the hemisphere of time to that of eternity! But though their names may be forgotten, their good works will remain, for "Good deed," as they say in India, "never dies."

DAYÂNANDA SARASVATI.

One more Samâj should be mentioned here to prevent confusion, namely, the Ârya-Samâj. This movement, which was inaugurated by another man, of the name of Dayânanda Sarasvatî, was proclaimed as a revival of the ancient Vedic religion. Dayânanda held fast to his belief in the Veda as a divine revelation, though he understood by Veda the hymns only, and admitted that the Brâhma*n*as showed clear traces of human workmanship. The followers of Dayânanda are quite aware that the Vedas were composed long before the art of writing was discovered in India, and they strongly object to the Veda being styled book-revelation, which they evidently consider as an inferior kind of revelation. They say, what they have no doubt learnt from European scholars, that the Vedas were not received in the form of books, but were revealed to the four principal Rishis. But their antagonists of the Brâhma-Samâj rejoin that, because the Vedas were committed to paper only a few thousand years back, it does not follow that they do not partake of the nature of book-revelation. They ask point blank whether Dayânanda and his followers believe that the very words and combinations of words forming the hymns of the Vedas as we now find them in MSS. were uttered by God himself? As long as they hold to this belief, the followers of Keshub Chunder Sen accuse them of being believers in book-revelation, quite as much as if they held that the bound volumes of the Veda had tumbled down from heaven. Their discussions on that point are often very ingenious, and may prove instructive even to our own apologists. Dayânanda himself and his followers disclaim any indebtedness to Western ideas, and they have gained many adherents, chiefly on the ground that, though pervaded by a reforming spirit, their Samâj has always remained thoroughly national. Dayânanda denounced idolatry and polytheism, he even repudiated caste, and allowed widow marriages. This required great courage, but, being a liberal conservative, he was naturally attacked both by liberals, for not going far enough, and by conservatives, for going too far. His followers believe that he was actually poisoned by his enemies. I am told that, at present, this revival of the ancient national religion has gained and is gaining far more support in India than the reforms initiated by Rammohun Roy and Keshub Chunder Sen. National feelings are strong in religious matters also. But though his doctrines may be more popular, there is more real vitality, more real reasonableness in the ideas of the other Brâhma-Samâjes. If they would only combine under a strong leader, they would, I believe, soon carry with them the wavering followers of Dayânanda; for in India whoever has once taken the first step, and surrendered his belief in the revealed character of even a part of the Veda, will easily be driven to take another step and adopt human reason as the only guide to human truth.

We know little of the personal character of Dayânanda, and what we know sounds very apocryphal. Though I was told soon after his death that he had been poisoned by the Brâhmans, who were afraid of his sweeping social reforms, I am now told by an Indian friend of mine that it is supposed that his death was caused by the dancing girls who, at the instigation of Dayânanda had been placed under strict *surveillance* by the Mahârâjah of Jayapura. Their stipends had been stopped, and they are supposed to have enticed a young Brâhman cook to poison their enemy. The cook is said to have afterwards committed suicide. This though only a rumour among rumours, would certainly put a different aspect on Dayânanda's sudden death. He must have been a powerful man, and he knew how to be a leader of men. His ignorance of English deprived him of much that would have been helpful to him, and would have kept him from some of his wild ideas about the Veda. He maintained that all wisdom was to be found in it, down to the discovery of the power of steam and its application to steam engines for railways; and this thousands of years B.C.! He was still more unfortunate in falling, for a time, an easy prey to Madame Blavatsky's spiritual fascinations.

For some time he understood her as little as she understood him, and that is saying a good deal. But when at last they came to understand each other, there followed a breach that could never be healed. The life of Dayânanda, published under the authority of the so-called Theosophists, which I accepted formerly as genuine, has been discredited, and we shall probably never have a real biography of the man, for biography in India seems to share the fate of history; either it tells us nothing, or what it tells us is fact and fiction so mixed together that it is impossible to separate the one from the other.

We can see clearly, however, that a strong and healthy fermentation is going on in the religious life of India, and if we consider the geographical extent of that country and the influence that it has always exercised on the intellectual atmosphere of the East, we can hardly treat that religious movement, which was inaugurated by Rammohun Roy, as indifferent to ourselves. What is wanting in it at present is the personal element, which is always very important in India. People are ready to be led, but they expect a leader to lead them.

I should never have understood the real motives and the true objects of these Indian reformers but for my personal intercourse with Dvârkanâth, years ago, and more recently with Keshub Chunder Sen. Though I did not know Rammohun Roy personally, I knew several of his friends who had known him at Bristol, and though I had no personal intercourse with Dayânanda, I learnt something of him also from some of his personal friends and followers. Still, we want to know a great deal more of the chief actors in the reformation which affects a far larger number of human beings than did the Reformation when it reinvigorated the whole of Europe in the sixteenth century. Some of the questions now being agitated in India are just the same as the questions which led in the end to the reformation of our own Church. If with us the chief question was that of the authority of the Bible replacing that of Pope and Councils, with them it is the authority of the Vedas. And if it was the first printed edition of the Greek New Testament by Erasmus that gave the strongest impulse to our Reformation, it was the first printed edition of the Veda that gave the most powerful incentive and the strongest weapon to the founders of the Brâhma-Samâj in India. Let us hope that India may be spared a Thirty Years' War before it can consolidate the work so courageously begun by Rammohun Roy, and so valiantly carried on by my departed friend, Keshub Chunder Sen.

It may very naturally be asked, but what is to

become of the religion of India, and more particularly of the religion of Keshub Chunder Sen and his friends and followers, after the very foundation of their ancient faith has been withdrawn, or, at all events, has been deprived of its sacred and infallible character? What would become of us if, say, by the discovery of ancient papyri in Egypt, it were suddenly placed beyond the reach of reasonable doubt that the Old and the New Testaments had been composed by some well-known Rabbi or philosopher in Egypt? Keshub Chunder Sen himself might have thought that all was gained after the heavy incubus of the Vedas had once been removed from his conscience; but some even of his best friends thought, not unnaturally, that all was lost. The idea that whatever truth was contained in the Vedas remained the same, whether with or without supernatural credentials, and that its acceptance without any such credentials required even a greater amount of honest conviction or faith than its acceptance on the ground of an assurance of its superhuman authorship, and that assurance given by human individuals like ourselves, seems never to have been entertained by the former believers in the Veda. To most of us the Bible would probably remain the same, whoever might be proved to have written it. But it was not so, as far as I can see, with the members of the Brâhma-Samâj. And yet it was felt that their Samâj or Church, if it was to strike root, required some kind of sacred code after the momentous decision had been taken to give up the Vedas. It must not be supposed that these reformers were without religion; on the contrary, they had more of the true religious spirit in them than those from whom they differed and from whom they had separated; and it was only the strength of their religious convictions that emboldened them to throw away their crutches and to stand without any intermediary, whether human or divine, before the highest object of their faith and veneration.

The first step they took was to explore some of the great religions of the world, and to select from their sacred books the most important and most convincing passages. This was very carefully done by Keshub Chunder Sen himself, but this international Bible failed to appeal to the hearts of the people of India. In religion anything that is not homegrown, or has become familiar to us from our childhood, cannot easily be divested of a strange and almost grotesque sound. When Bishop Colenso published an English translation of a beautiful prayer addressed to Vish*n*u, it produced nothing but merriment among his English readers, and why? Because Vish*n*u was addressed in it by his well-known popular name of Hari, and the invocation "O Harry" was too much for the risible muscles of John Bull.

The same effect was produced on the Hindus when they were told of a God that had made the world in six days, and rested the seventh day, or when they heard Christ invoked as *Agnus Dei*, or Vatsa Devasya. Language is a very important element in religion, and the slightest incongruity is sometimes fatal. It is well known that Dr. Arnold had to part with an excellent French master at Rugby simply because he had spoken of the Holy Ghost as a pigeon, instead of a dove. The boys could never forget or forgive it.

Then there was also the national sentiment, which asserts itself, even when it seems to be most out of place. The people of India wanted to have a national religion, and they did not see why they should have to borrow their prayers from Jews, Christians, Parsis, or other infidels. I strongly advised Keshub Chunder Sen, when he was staying with me at Oxford, to have a good translation made of the New Testament in Sanskrit, and in the more important vernaculars of India, only leaving out the historical passages, which conveyed no meaning to the large masses of the people in India, and any other chapters or verses which he considered inappropriate for influencing the Indian mind. Keshub himself was quite ready to adopt such a course, for he was really in his heart a true follower of Christ. Once when I had asked him why he did not declare himself publicly a Christian, he said, in a very grave and thoughtful tone, "Suppose that thirty years hence people find out that I was a disciple of Christ, what would be the harm? Only were I to profess myself a Christian now, all my influence would be gone at once." Whether any steps were taken by Keshub to carry out the idea of a New Testament for India I cannot tell. Something of the same kind had been done in English by Rammohun Roy himself. The book has become very scarce, and I doubt whether it ever influenced even his own followers.

Debendranâth Tagore, the paternal friend of Keshub Chunder Sen, adopted a different course. He would never declare against the whole Veda, but, discarding the hymns and the Brâhma*n*as, he made a careful selection of important passages from the Upanishads, and published them, with an explanation in Sanskrit, under the title of "Brâhma-dharma," the Law of the Brâhmas. This became for a time the new guide of the Brâhmas, even before Keshub Chunder Sen published his selections from the Bibles of the world, and will probably in time become their Bible, or at all events their Book of Meditations. The primitive religious doctrines of the Upanishads were reduced to an elaborate system of philosophy by Bâdarâya*n*a, probably long before the Christian era, though after the rise of Buddhism (fifth century), under the title of Vedânta-Sûtras, and a most wonderful system it is, though difficult to describe in a few pages. It is generally supposed that the Vedânta philosophy denies the reality of the whole world. But this is not so; it only declares, and even more consistently than we do, that the world is phenomenal. It is not what it seems to be, but it would not even seem to be, unless it reposed on the Divine, which alone is really real. That Divine, in order to be what it is, or what it ought to be conceived to be, must, according to the Vedânta, be free from all limitation, it must therefore be one, with nothing beside it, it must be subjective, not objective or perceptible by the senses, devoid therefore of all qualities. But, instead of calling the world a mere nothing, the old Vedântists held, on the contrary, that there could be nothing objective or phenomenal, unless there was something real beneath it, in comparison with which anything else might be called unreal, that is, phenomenal. Thus, even our unreal world could not exist unless there was at the back of it a something real; and, if we claim any reality for ourselves, we can only do so after surrendering all that is phenomenal in ourselves, all that is changing, perishing, and mortal. Only then can we find and recover our true being, where alone it can be found, namely in the divine, invisible, but ever-present, absolute Power, the uncreate, the eternal and never-changing Being whom we call God. This was that ultimate Reality which they called Brahman, and this was, in fact, but another name for what European philosophers have called the Ultimate, the Unknowable, the Great Reality, the Hidden, the Abyss, the Silence, the Fulness, the Eternal Life—names all meaning the same, or meant for the same, though powerless to reach what is beyond the reach of words.

Then came the very natural question, whence comes the change from the Real to the Phenomenal, or what we call the creation? Whence the phenomenal in place of the noumenal world? The Vedânta answer is, From Nescience. This has been called the weak, the human, the vulnerable point in the Vedânta; but we should remember that, in some shape or other, that vulnerable point can never be absent from any system of philosophy. I doubt whether there are many founders of philosophies who have disguised it better than Bâdarâyan*a* and his predecessors in the Upanishads. Nescience, they say, is neither real nor unreal. It is, but it cannot be called real, because it can be destroyed, and is to be destroyed by Vidyâ, science, i. e. the Vedânta philosophy; yet it cannot be called unreal, for we see its effects in all the phenomenal world. This Nescience must not be taken for the ignorance of the individual man, or for his unacquaintance with the Vedânta philosophy. It is something inherent in human nature. Brahman itself is affected by it indirectly, but not directly. Brahman, as conceived by us, may be said to be for a time under its sway. A power such as this nescience was sure to yield to the mythopoeic influence of language, and to become *she*, as it did under the name of Mâyâ (illusion, magic), or even of *S*akti, *potentia*.

But whether that impulse which produced the phenomenal world is called Avidyâ (nescience), or Mâyâ (illusion), or *S*akti (potentia), it was and is the aim of Vidyâ or the Vedânta philosophy to dispel it, and thus to destroy the illusion that there is any real difference between man and Brahman. It then becomes clear that this phenomenal world in its endless variety is but an ignorance, a dream that will pass away, if once our eyes are opened. Whatever is known by us, becomes, *ipso facto*, objective and phenomenal, and to know this is the first step towards the truth. It may seem difficult to understand how such a philosophy could be treated as orthodox, and go hand in hand with the popular religion. But we must remember that Brahman, the first and the only real Being, as soon as perceived or conceived as an object, becomes at once a phenomenal being. Thus Brahman (neut.) became to human intelligence Brahmâ (masc.), and was recognised and worshipped as phenomenalised under such popular names as *S*iva, Vish*n*u, Kr*i*sh*n*a, and many more. In this way the old mythological gods had not to be discarded altogether; on the contrary, devotion to them (Bhakti) was not only tolerated, but actually enjoined, till true knowledge or *Gñ*âna had arisen. *S*iva and Vish*n*u and other gods were accepted as persons or as faces (Pratîka) of Brahman. Nay, they were recognised as the phenomena of Brahman, and whosoever worshipped them was led to believe that he worshipped Brahman, though ignorantly. Here lies a wonderful amount of wisdom, from which even we may have something to learn; and it is not surprising that some of these modern Hindu philosophers and religious teachers should have felt that they had not only to learn from us, but had something also to teach us. This may sound very strange to our ears, and yet what is more natural? Nay, strange as it sounds to our ears, it is nevertheless a fact, that may have been exaggerated in the American papers, but that is not without some real foundation, namely, that some Vedântist missionaries, such as Vivekânanda, Abhedânanda, *S*âradânada, and others, who were sent to America, are lecturing there before large audiences, and have actually made some converts who accept the Vedântic view of the world, and call themselves Theosophists or Vedântists. These missionaries are mostly the disciples and followers of a well-known Indian ascetic, who had spent his life in preaching Vedântic sentiments, and who died as late as 1886.* Men of that class are well known in India, and are spoken of as Mahâtmans. They live as much as possible retired from the world, it may be in a cave or a small hut in the forest. They wear hardly anything but rags, bear heat, cold, and hunger without complaining, and strive hard to become Vairâgins, men without any passions and without any desires. It need hardly be said that some of them are mere impostors and disreputable characters, well known to the police. Others, however, are real religious enthusiasts. Though they may know a little Sanskrit, they are not the recognised depositaries of ancient learning; but, once filled and fired with the spirit of the Vedânta, they become very eloquent preachers, and gather crowds around them, willing to drink in the

* A full account of this Saint is to be found in a book lately published by me, "Râmak*r*ish*n*a, his Life and Sayings," by F. M. M., 1898.

truths which never fail to exercise their intoxicating power on the Indian mind. Many of these Mahâtmans know by long practice how to put themselves into a real trance, and thus to make people believe that they have been outside their body or beside themselves, and have received inspirations from a divine source. If this is a deception, it is certainly a very old deception. It is practised by sons, as they had seen it practised by their fathers, and, as far as I can see, without any sinister intentions. Râmak*ri*sh*n*a and men of his class are addicted to Bhakti, devotion or love, rather than to *Gñ*âna, knowledge, or pure philosophy. They speak of K*ri*sh*n*a rather than of Brahman, nay, Brahman itself becomes with them Brahmâ, a masculine and active god. If some of these men declare their perfect willingness to adopt the religion of Christ, they can do so with perfect honesty. The God of Christianity, the Creator of the world, the Father of all the children of man, would be to them but another name, another face or person of the Godhead. Christ would be to them not simply a manifestation, like Râma or Nârada, but, from a far higher point of view, born of God, one with God, having realised God, as we all are to realise Him in time, in order to attain real brotherhood with Christ and among ourselves, and divine sonship, the long forgotten or forfeited birthright of every son of man. Would not that be enough to make them Christians, truer Christians than even some of the missionaries, who approach them as if they were a degraded race, and who are often satisfied if they can baptize them, even without having really converted them? If we want them to understand us, let us first try to understand them. If that mutual recognition is once achieved, there may be a future for Christianity in store in India such as we hardly venture to dream of as yet. There are Hindus of the highest caste who would be able, like the eunuch, to say with perfect honesty that they believe that Jesus Christ was the son of God, in the highest sense of the word. What then hindereth them to be baptized? No wonder that European visitors who come to see these devotees in India should often be repelled by what they see. They are generally naked, or in rags, with dishevelled hair, emaciated, and not always very clean. Their expression is wild and often half crazy. Even their photographs are enough to frighten us. But for all that, their utterances, partly their own, partly echoes of what they have heard, are sometimes very powerful and even beautiful, and people of all classes, educated and uneducated, are willing to listen to them for hours. One thing is certainly to their credit. Though they accept alms, they never ask for them;

and even the missionaries who have travelled all the way to America to lecture and preach, never ask for money. They do not want it, and what is given to them is sent to India forthwith towards a fund for building and endowing what we should call monasteries, where the style of life is as simple as it was in the best days of monastic life in Europe. The sayings of Râmakr*i*sh*n*a have been published by his disciples, and I cannot resist the temptation of giving here at least a few of them :—

"Thou seest many stars at night in the sky, but findest them not when the sun rises. Canst thou say that there are no stars then in the heaven of day? O man, because thou beholdest not the Almighty in the days of thy ignorance, say not that there is no God."

"Different creeds are but different paths to reach the Almighty."

"As from the same gold various ornaments are made, having different forms and names, so our God is worshipped in different countries and ages, and has different forms and names. Though He may be worshipped variously, some loving to call Him Father, others Mother &c., yet it is one God that is being worshipped in all these various relations and modes."

"Man is like a cushion-cover. The colour of one may be red, another blue, another black, but all contain the same cotton inside. So it is with man ; one is beautiful, one is black, another holy, a fourth wicked; but the Divine dwells in all of them."

"God is in all men, but all men are not in God, that is the reason why they suffer."

"As the lamp does not burn without oil, man cannot live without God."

"There are two egos in man, one ripe and the other unripe. The ripe ego thinks, 'Nothing is mine, whatever I see, or feel, or hear, nay, even this body is not mine; I am always free and eternal.' The unripe ego, on the contrary, thinks, 'This is my house, my room, my child, my wife, my body,' &c."

"When the knowledge of Self is obtained, all fetters fall off by themselves. Then there is no distinction of a Brâhmana or a *S*ûdra, of high caste or low caste. In that case the sacred thread, the sign of caste, falls away of itself. But so long as man has the consciousness of distinction and difference of caste, he should not forcibly throw it away."

"A man after fourteen years of hard asceticism in a lonely forest, obtained at last the power of walking on the waters. Overjoyed at this acquisition, he went to his teacher and told him of his great feat. At this the master replied: 'My poor boy, what thou hast accomplished after fourteen years of arduous labour, ordinary men do the same by paying a penny to the boatman.'"

"Where is God? How can we get at Him? There are pearls in the sea. One must dive again and again till one gets at them. So there is God in the world, but you should persevere in diving."

"The vanities of all others may gradually die out, but the vanity of a saint is hard, indeed, to wear away."

There are hundreds of such sayings all breathing the same spirituality, the same familiarity with the unseen world. Some of them sound to us trivial and common, but in publishing them I did not like to leave out any, for fear of being suspected of falsifying the record and representing the bright side of the movement only. To our taste there may be too much of that familiarity. Silence in the presence of God seems to us more reverential than words, but to a man of the character of Râmak*ri*sh*n*a, and I might say, to Hindus in general, the distance between the human and the Divine, between God and man, has always been very small, till at last it seems to vanish altogether. To their eyes the unseen world and the unseen God are not unseen. The veil formed by what we call the flesh is to them so transparent that it often vanishes altogether. The idea of a distance from God or of a gradual approach to Him after death exists indeed in their exoteric philosophy, but to the true Vedântist such an approach is really unthinkable. To the Vedântist the highest goal has always been to have his humanity taken back into the Godhead, not to put on a new nature, but to recover his old and true nature, in fact to become what, in spite of the dreams and fancies of life, he has always been. Those who cannot soar so high, may indeed be allowed to worship a distant God, nay, to approach his throne reverentially in another life, and they are taught that even in that state of mind, they are moving forward on the right road, the road that may at last bring them to themselves and make them enjoy the Divine and the Eternal within them. Hence with all their strong sense of the imperfections of this life, with the acknowledgment of their guilt and their consequent separation from God, they never use the disparaging language of other religions which seems to make man the most contemptible worm on earth. No doubt, they also have imagined a number of beings intermediate between God and man, but when these creatures of their own fancy have been dissolved again, they seem to feel that in reality there is no class of real beings that can claim to fill the self-made gap between God and man. Râmak*ri*sh*n*a himself was still in the bonds of the popular faith of India. He worshipped the gods created by man, such as Vish*n*u, *S*iva, and others, he did not shrink even from offering sacrifices to idols, but he felt and saw that behind them there is the inexpressible Essence which is more than any or all of them. The purely human devotion and love which he expresses for his Divine Mother, for instance, is sometimes most startling, but one feels all the time that, if he could only express it, he is groping for that Godhead which he must find in himself or in his Self before he can find it in the Self of the whole world, in the Self even of the old idols. A distant God like the Jewish Jehovah would be no God at all to the Vedântist, he cannot be too near to his God; nay, to be without Him but for one moment would be death and annihilation to him.

Such ideas are no doubt strange to most of us, but if we cannot as yet make them our own, we should at all events give Râmak*ri*sh*n*a and his followers credit for holding them honestly.

MY INDIAN FRIENDS

III

BEHRAMJI MALABÂRI

INTIMATELY connected with the reform of religion in India were social reforms, such as the education of women, the recognition of widow-marriages, the fixing of the marriageable age of boys and girls, &c. The burning of widows or of Suttees, had been boldly put down by the English Government years ago; though, as we saw, it was still defended as resting on Vedic authority by so learned and enlightened a man as Râdhâkânta Deva. But, though widows were no longer burnt, their life as widows was in many cases worse than death. Owing to the system of very early, and what has been truly called, child-marriages, the number of child-widows is, and has been for many years, very large in India; and the only means of reducing their number was to prohibit early marriages altogether. The chief actors in this good work were my friend Behramji Malabâri, and another dear friend, Râmabâi, both still alive and hard at work in the good cause. The former was chiefly bent on preventing these premature marriages, the latter on taking care of the victims of that pernicious system. We need not enter here on purely physiological questions, for here the answer is always ready that marriage at the early age of seven or eight can mean no more than betrothal. That in the East, men and women are more precocious in their physical development is an assertion rather than an established fact. But it is not the body only, it is the mind that has to be considered, and what can be the mental condition of a child-wife of seven, nay, even of fourteen? How such a system ever sprang up, it is difficult to say. It was not the old Indian system. It may have originated at the time of the Mohammedan conquest, married women being supposed to be more respected by the conquerors than unmarried girls. At present its fatal effects are but too clear, in the premature decay of the women, in the weakness of their offspring, and, more particularly, in the large number of child-widows. No wonder therefore that a man of Malabâri's patriotism and sense of duty should have devoted himself body and soul, and purse too, to the abolition of that evil. Though there were many to sympathise with him and to help him, still there was also strong opposition, and from quarters where one would least have expected it. Malabâri was a Parsi, and the Hindus did not like to be lectured by an outsider. If their dirty linen had to be washed at all, they wished to have it washed at home by their own washerwomen. Others, though admitting abuses, gave a most idyllic picture of the first love of young children, which extended its blessing over the whole of their lives, while the European system led to endless misery, to broken hearts, to divided affections, and sometimes even to a sundering of ties which in the eyes of the Hindus can never be sundered.

There have been many strong protests from numbers of well-conducted families in India who deny altogether that child-widows, or any widows, are subject to cruel treatment, and who maintain that early marriages have by no means all the evil effects which are charged against them. There are exceptions, no doubt, to everything, but I doubt whether these exceptions can make up for the mischief caused by the system of early marriages as still prevalent in India. And what is there that can be urged in favour of a system which even its strongest supporters can only defend as less monstrous than it appears to be. We are told * that in Bengal a young husband is able to educate his young wife. That sounds very well. But in a Hindu family a married child is not supposed even to see her husband during the daytime, so

* The Interpreter, November, 1898, p. 303.

that the education, whatever that may mean, could only take place in the stillness of the night, not the most propitious time after a day of constant work. We are likewise told that a child-wife divides her year in two halves. One of them she spends with her parents, this being a sort of vacation time, and the other she spends at the house of her husband's parents, this being confessedly the time of daily drudgery. In well-ordered families the young wife is never allowed to live with her husband permanently till she has reached her fourteenth year.

This defence, however, does not amount to much, and though we may quite believe that in good families the evils of the system of child-marriage are very much mitigated, the system itself is unnatural, full of dangers, and certainly lowering, both physically and morally, to the mothers of India.

The most unexpected defender of child-marriages appeared in Ânandibâi Joshee, a young Hindu lady who had gone to America to study medicine, and, after taking her medical degree at the Women's Medical College of Pennsylvania in 1886, was appointed Physician-in-Charge of the Female Ward of the Albert-Edward Hospital at Kolhapur, and died in 1887 at the early age of twenty-two. She was evidently a most enlightened lady, and a great friend of Râmabâi. But when she had been asked, in 1884, to lecture on child-marriages, she surprised her large American audience by defending the national custom of early marriage. I am sorry I have never been able to hear her lecture, but it shows at all events that the abolition of that custom was not so universally desired as it ought to have been, and by no means so easy in India as it might appear to us. We are told that the early betrothal of boys and girls made their mutual affection more natural and firm, and added the feelings of brother and sister to those of husband and wife. It was fondly hoped that under such circumstances the idea of anybody else ever taking the place of the first beloved one would be altogether impossible. Many other arguments were adduced in support of what seemed a national, time-hallowed, and almost sacred custom, but they soon crumbled away at the touch of so well-informed and determined a man as my friend Malabâri. I do not know how many voyages he has made to England to insure sympathy and help. He has spent years in travelling all over India and gaining support for his crusade. He has told us that he is a poor man, but whatever he possessed or gained, he seems to have given up for the main object of his life. I am quite willing to believe that in the better families the evil consequences of premature matrimony are guarded against, just as I cannot altogether withhold my belief from those who declare that in good families child-widows, and in fact all widows, are treated with sympathy and respect. But without denying such exceptions, it was the rule or the custom, such as he knew it to exist, that roused the indignation of Malabâri. He may be congratulated on having lived to see some at least of the fruits of his devoted labours. Assisted by his friends, both native and English, he carried at last a Bill which fixed the respective ages of freedom to marry at eighteen and twelve. This was a decided victory; still the battle is by no means over, and probably never will be till the marriageable age of girls is raised at least to sixteen, and that of boys to twenty. It was twenty-four in Vedic times. That every kind of abuse was heaped on Malabâri need not surprise us; still his own conscience must tell him that he has done a real service to millions of human beings, and removed from his country a slur that had lowered it in the eyes of all civilised nations. It is highly creditable to him that he declined all rewards and honours offered to him at the end of his successful campaign, and we should not be surprised if we met him again on the old battlefield, anxious to win new victories as the defender of a good cause.

9

The number of widows in India is simply appalling. According to the census of the year 1881 their number of all ages amounted, at that time, to twenty million nine hundred and thirty thousand six hundred and twenty-six. Of these six hundred and sixty-nine thousand one hundred were under nineteen years of age.

From 15 to 19 years of age	382,736
From 10 to 14 years of age	207,388
Under 9 years of age	78,976
	669,100

Even native states have taken up the cause of the unhappy children. Some of the Rajput states some years ago declared against premature marriage, and Mysore has now followed their good example, passing a law not only to prevent child-marriages, but to make it penal for an old man to marry a young girl. I doubt whether such a law would pass even our own Parliament. Clause 3 says:—

> Any person who causes the marriage of a girl who has not completed fourteen years of age, with a man who has completed fifty years of age, and any person who knowingly aids and abets, within the meaning of the Indian Penal Code, such marriage, shall be punished with simple imprisonment for a term which may extend to six months, or with fine, or with both.

The Madras Presidency will now have to follow the example of Mysore, instead of taking the lead, as it ought to have done. In a Memorandum accompanying the Bill for the Madras Presidency, it is stated that in 1882 there were 157,466 girls married under the age of nine, and that there were 5,621 widows under the same age. Think of widows under nine years of age!

In the census of 1891 it was shown that there were 23,938 girls married in their fourth year and under, and 142,606 between five and nine years of age, giving a total of 166,544 girls married under nine years of age. There were 988 widows of four years and under, and 4,147 between five and nine years, making a total of 5,135. In future, however, the law is never to recognise any widows under nine years of age, and there is every hope that the number of these baby-widows will be considerably reduced as soon as no girl can be betrothed till she has reached, at least, the age of eight; the bridegroom being, as a rule, five or six years older. This is, of course, much too low an age, but it was considered the least likely to rouse opposition among the native population, as some of the law-books of the Hindus are in favour of that age, while they actually threaten parents who do not marry their daughter before ten with the hell called Raurava. The greatest living legal authorities in

India have declared in favour of a limit of age, fixing it at eight for girls. As their support gives immense strength to the aspirations of the reform party, its leaders have accepted it for the present. Men like Malabâri are of course not satisfied, yet they may be proud to have achieved what they have achieved. They have at all events reduced the number of possible child-widows, by limiting the marriageable age of girls to eight. Much more, however, remains to be done, and Malabâri is not the man to let sleeping dogs lie. He wields a powerful pen in English, and he is the best living writer of Guzerathi. He began life as a Guzerathi poet, but he gave up poetry and everything else to concentrate all his energy on his crusade. He has written several very successful English books, the last being "The Indian Eye on English Life." He is the editor of an influential paper at Bombay, *The Indian Spectator*. He has also undertaken to spread my Hibbert Lectures "On the Origin and Growth of Religion" all over India, by having them translated into Sanskrit and every one of the modern languages of the country. This undertaking also he has carried through successfully, without flinching from considerable trouble and pecuniary risk. All these undertakings require money, and in the present state of things a willingness to spend money is a very good, if not the best, test of a man's sincerity. Malabâri has stood that test for many years, and much as he longs for rest, I learn that he is not likely to stand by with folded arms, and to leave the fight to others.*

RÂMABÂI.

If we admire the boldness and perseverance of Malabâri, we cannot withhold the same admiration from a young Indian lady who, though she could not hope to prevent child-marriages, has done her very best to ameliorate the lot of the victims of those unnatural unions.

To be a widow at all is hard enough, but nothing can be more miserable than the lot of a young widow in India, whose life may be said to be over before it has begun. Widows are looked upon in their own homes as beings of evil omen, as having deserved their misfortune by some unknown misdeeds in this or, what is worse, in a former life, and, particularly if childless, they are treated no better than servants, whether in the house of their parents-in-law, or even in the house of their real parents, if they are allowed to return there. They are shunned, excluded from all amusements, obliged to wear coarse garments, deprived of their ornaments, and often condemned to have their

* See an excellent account of his life by Karkaria.

heads shaved, a great indignity in the eyes of every woman. What a life to look forward to for a girl, often, it may be, not yet sixteen years old! No wonder that they should often commit suicide, or fall still lower by being driven to lead an immoral life. It is to ameliorate the lot of these unhappy creatures that Râmabâi has been working for years, chiefly at Poonah. She is certainly a most courageous woman, not to be turned away from her purpose by any misfortunes or any threats.

I saw much of her when she stayed with us at Oxford, but the most eventful part of her career belonged to an earlier period. With what she told me then, and what has been published since by Mrs. R. L. Bodley in the Introduction to Râmabâi's account of the "Life of a High-Caste Hindu Woman" (Philadelphia, 1887), we begin to understand the high aims of this truly heroic Hindu lady, in appearance small, delicate, and timid, but in reality strong and bold as a lioness. Her life, so far as we know it from herself and from others, draws away the veil behind which so much that is really of the deepest interest to us, is hidden in the East. Here we see first of all from her own case how carelessly marriages are often arranged in India. Râmabâi's grandfather, who belonged to an old and very illustrious Brahmanic family, the Kauthumas, was on a religious pilgrimage with his family, that is, his wife and two daughters, one nine, the other seven years of age. One morning, when bathing in the Godâvarî, he saw a fine-looking man in the river, and after inquiring for his caste, his clan, and his home, and finding out that he was a widower, he offered him his eldest daughter, that is, a child of nine, in marriage. All things being satisfactorily settled in a few hours, the marriage took place the next day, and the stranger started with his child-wife for his home, nearly nine hundred miles away from the child's own home, while the father continued his pilgrimage, unconcerned any longer about the fate of his daughter. However, the marriage, though we might call it hasty and imprudent, turned out well, and her husband, who was a great Sanskrit scholar, a pupil of Râmachandra *S*âstri, not only was kind to his little wife, but was most anxious to teach her the sacred language. This was a very unusual measure, in fact, it was against the Brahmanic law. It seems that he had made the same experiment with his first wife, but that it had failed owing to the opposition of her family. When therefore he was met by a similar opposition in the case of his second wife, he suddenly left his home and his friends, and journeyed with his young wife to the forest of Gungamul, on a remote plateau of the Western Ghauts, and there founded his new home, where the world could no longer hinder or trouble him. Such things are possible in India only, and even there they are of rare occurrence. Râmabâi was told by her mother how she and her husband spent the first night after their flight from home in the open air without shelter of any kind, she rolled up in her pasodi or cotton quilt, he watching by her side. Wild animals were heard howling all around them, and the young wife lay convulsed with terror; and no wonder she did, though her husband kept watch till day-break, frightening the wild animals away as best he could from his bride and his new home. However, there, in the forest, husband and wife, like another Yâ*gn*avalkya and Maitreyî, remained, and there the husband began to teach his wife Sanskrit. A rude hut was soon constructed, such as suffices in a forest and in the climate of India. The wife grew in stature and in knowledge, and soon became the mother of three children born in this wilderness, one son and two daughters. As they grew up the father at once began the instruction of his son and his elder daughter. Soon the fame of his scholarship began to attract other students from the neighbourhood, and the hermitage, situated as it was near the source of one of the rivers, became a place of pilgrimage, and attracted many visitors.

When the younger daughter, our Râmabâi, grew

up, the father was getting too old and too weary to teach her also, so that her education fell chiefly to the share of her mother, Lakshmâbâi.

Soon the household grew, partly by the arrival of the aged father and mother-in-law, who had to be taken care of, partly by the arrival of many pilgrims, who in India have a right to hospitable entertainment. At last the expenses grew too high, the little hermitage had to be broken up, and father and children had to begin a new life, that of a pilgrim family without any home, wandering about from place to place, tramping, in fact, as we should say, and earning a small livelihood by recitations, whether in palaces or monasteries. When Râmabâi began her career as a prodigy of learning, she had learned ever so many Sanskrit texts by heart, either from her mother or from listening unknown, as she told me, to the lessons given by her father to her brother. Erudition in India means learning by heart. A pupil learns a number of verses every day and repeats them the next day, constantly adding new lines, till at last he can repeat thousands of lines without a hitch. Râmabâi listened at the door while her brother and other students repeated their daily lessons, and in this way she learnt in the end to repeat more lines than most young Brâhmans. For this she received rewards while travelling on foot from place to place with her father, mother, and brother. The elder sister had been married, though not very happily, it would seem, while Râmabâi gladly remained unmarried long after the statutable age. This was really considered as a breach of the law, but as long as her parents were alive she had a recognised support in them. When, however, the father died, and very soon after the mother also, her position became almost desperate. She still had her brother, who then became her natural guardian and protector; but the whole of the small family property had been spent. There was not even enough left to pay a few Brâhmans for carrying the remains of her mother to the burning-ghat, about three miles distant. At last two Brâhmans were found who took pity on the bereaved children, and with their assistance son and daughter carried the sacred burden to the place of cremation. Poor Râmabâi's low stature compelled her to carry her share of the dear burden on her head. We can hardly imagine such a state of things, and such suffering; yet what seems to us incredible comes from Râmabâi's own mouth, and, from what I know of her, she may be implicitly trusted. When I once asked her how she knew that she belonged to the famous Brâhmanic clan of the Kauthumas, she replied very simply, "But who would ever doubt it?" And the same remark applies to all that she has told us of the sufferings of her life.

These sufferings were not over yet. She had now no one to look to but her brother, and without some male support the life of a single woman is simply impossible in India. For some years brother and sister travelled together on foot all over India, earning what they wanted for their support by their recitations of Sanskrit texts, and afterwards by lecturing on the degraded position of women in India. Arrived in Calcutta Râmabâi's lectures excited great interest. But now followed a new blow. Her brother died, and from sheer necessity she had to take a husband. The marriage turned out perfectly happy, but after nineteen months of quiet married life there followed a new blow. Her husband died, and she was left a widow with one daughter, whom she called Manoramâ, or Heart's Joy.

Her case seemed desperate indeed, but she was upheld by her strong desire to fit herself for useful work among her own countrywomen. Helpless as she was, she resolved to go to England in order to study medicine. This was a bold decision, and required more moral courage than Napoleon's march to Russia.

Member of a high-caste Brâhman family though she was, the mere prejudice against crossing the black water would hardly have affected her, but she was very poor. All she possessed was a small sum of money which she had earned by her lectures and by translations done for Government, and how was she to pay for her passage and to support herself, her child, and a friend who was to accompany her to England? But undeterred by any fears she started with her little daughter and a female friend, and when she arrived in England, almost destitute, she fortunately found shelter for a time with the Sisterhood at Wantage, some members of which she had known at Poonah. But even then her tragedy was not yet ended. She had declared to the Sisters that, grateful as she felt for their kindness, she would never become a Christian, because, as she often said, a good Brâhma*n*î is quite as good as a good Christian. Her friend, however, was frightened by the idea that she and Râmabâi would be made Christians by force; and to save Râmabâi and herself from such a fate, she tried one night to strangle her. Failing in that, she killed herself. It was after this terrible catastrophe at Wantage that Râmabâi came to stay with us at Oxford, and such was her nervous prostration that we had to give her a maidservant to sleep every night in the same room with her. Nor was this all. After all arrangements had been made to enable her to attend medical lectures at Oxford, her hearing became suddenly so much affected that she had to give up all idea of a medical career. She then determined to study nursing, and thus fit herself for useful work in India. Then came an invitation from America to be present at the conferring of a medical degree on her countrywoman, Ânandibâi Joshee, of whom I spoke before, and being once there, she soon succeeded in gaining many friends, who helped her to start a refuge or Âsrama for child-widows in India. This is the work to which at last she has devoted herself, and with great success, her only difficulty being that in the meantime she had, after all, become a Christian and joined her Christian friends; not that she considered her former religion false or mischievous, but because, as she told me, she could no longer stand quite alone, she wanted to belong to somebody, and particularly to be able to worship together with those whom she loved and who had been so kind to her. Her having become a Christian has, no doubt, proved a serious obstacle to her success in her chosen sphere of usefulness in India. Though we may trust her that she never made an attempt at proselytising among the little widows committed to her care, yet how could it be otherwise than that those to whom the world had been so unkind, and Râmabâi so kind, should wish to be what their friend was, Christian! Her goodness was the real proselytising power that could not be hidden; but she lost, of course, the support of her native friends, and has even now to fight her battles alone, in order to secure the pecuniary assistance necessary for the support of her little army of child-widows. She is, indeed, a noble and unselfish woman, and deserves every help which those who sympathise with her objects, can afford to give her.

ÂNANDIBÂI JOSHEE, M.D.

There is another Hindu lady to whom I alluded before as a friend of Râmabâi's, who in fact invited Râmabâi to come to the United States to be present at her taking her degree of M.D. in the Medical College of Pennsylvania, and who thus determined, to a great extent, the future course of Râmabâi's life. She too must have been a young heroine, and it is well that her name should not be forgotten on the roll of martyrs, who have lived, worked, and died in the cause of elevating and regenerating their country. I draw my information chiefly from a sympathetic article, signed Isabel M. Sulivan, in the *Indian Social Reformer*, July 10, 1898. Ânandibâi was different from Râmabâi in one respect. Though free from many prejudices, she remained a true Brâhma*n*î through life. She fearlessly stood by Râmabâi after her husband's death, and even offered her the shelter of her home. She remained her faithful friend to the end, which took place in 1887, when she was only twenty-two years of age. Though she could not bring herself to go quite so far as Râmabâi in giving up the religion of her childhood, her enthusiasm took another, yet very perilous form. She had seen the untold physical sufferings of girls and women in India, who are almost entirely left to the medical care of uneducated *femmes sages* and inefficient nurses. But for a young girl of eighteen, brought up in the narrowly guarded sphere of an Indian home, to dream of leaving her country, to travel to America, and enter as a medical student at an American University required such an amount of moral courage as we should never have expected from a young and timid Hindu lady who could know little of the world outside her Zenânah, and had probably never spoken to a man except her husband and members of her own family. She was married already, when she conceived her plan of going to America, and such was her strength of character that she succeeded in persuading her husband to accompany her in her voyage of discovery, and to support her in her endeavour to preserve her caste while living abroad.

"I will go to America as a Hindu," she said, "and come back and live among my people as a Hindu." And she carried out her resolve in spite of endless difficulties. Yes, she had been married in 1874, at the age of nine. We can hardly believe in such marriages, yet they exist, and in her case this early, nay premature marriage proved certainly most successful. No wonder therefore that, when she was asked to speak about child-marriages before an American audience, she should have stood up for them, even in the presence of her friend Râmabâi, treating them, of course, as what they really are, betrothals, but betrothals binding for life. Accompanied by her husband, Gopalrao Vinayak Joshee, she arrived in the United States, being really the first Brâhman lady who had ever set foot in New York. From thence she went to Philadelphia, where her arrival is described to us by her friend, Dr. Rachel Bodley. "One day in September, 1883," she writes, "there came to my door a little lady in a blue cotton saree, accompanied by her faithful friend, Mrs. B. F. Carpenter of New Jersey, and since that hour, when, speechless for very wonder, I bestowed a kiss of welcome upon the stranger's cheek instead of words, I have loved the women of India. The little lady was Mrs. Ânandibâi Joshee, who had come to study medicine in the Medical College of Pennsylvania."

Dr. Bodley proved a true friend in need to the lonely stranger. She tells us that "though from the first Ânandibâi had received a cordial welcome in America, it must have been with some heart-sinking that she settled down alone in her college rooms, confronted by the anthracite coal stove, which was the only means of cooking her food, and which she did not know how to manage. She tried faithfully to prosecute her studies, and at the same time keep caste-rules and cook her own food, but the anthracite coal stove in her room was a constant vexation and likewise a source of danger, and the solitude of the individual house-keeping was overwhelming. After a trial of two weeks her health declined to such an alarming extent that I invited her to pay a short visit to my home, and she never left it again to dwell elsewhere in Philadelphia during her student-residence. In the performance of College duties, going in and out, up and down, always in her measured, quiet, dignified, patient way, she has filled every room with memories which now hallow the home and must continue to do so throughout the years to come." Ânandibâi's faculties developed rapidly under Western opportunities, her scientific acquirements placed her high in rank among her peers in College, and on March 11, 1886, she took her medical degree, being the first Hindu woman to receive the

Degree of Doctor of Medicine in any country. On June 1, 1886, she was appointed to the position of Physician-in-Charge of the Female Ward of the Albert Edward Hospital at Kolhapur, and on October 9 she sailed from New York to assume the duties of her new official position. But, alas, the strain of the last three years in a foreign land had undermined her constitution, perchance the cold of the American winters had attacked lungs inured to naught but tropical heat, and when she landed in Bombay it was found that she was in an advanced stage of consumption. She had come home to die, and, after spending three years in the study of medicine, she must have known very well the fate that awaited her. After these three years of voluntary exile, she found herself once more in the familiar places of her childhood, at Poonah, surrounded by her mother and sisters, and it was her mother's sad privilege to support her daughter in her arms when at midnight the end came quickly. This occurred on February 26, 1887, in the home in which she was born.

All this is unspeakably sad. So much silent heroism, so many sacrifices patiently borne for years, and then at the end resignation, and farewell! Mrs. Bodley, who has been such a motherly friend both to Ânandibâi and Râmabâi, and to whom we owe most of what we have been allowed to know of Ânandibâi's last years, when receiving the photograph of her protégée taken on her death-bed, writes: "The pathos of that lifeless form is indescribable. The last of several pictures taken during the brief public career of the little reformer, it is the most eloquent of them all. The mute lips, and the face wan and wasted and prematurely aged in the fierce battle with sorrow and pain alike convey to her American friends this message, not to be forgotten: 'I have done what I could.'"

If we consider all the impediments that barred the way of a young Indian lady when conceiving the plan of studying medicine in a foreign country, we are amazed at Ânandibâi's courage and perseverance, and we shall hesitate before we declare that Hindu women cannot be worthy peers of English women. Our own lady Doctors, who have cut their way through the compact phalanx of prejudice and jealousy, can best judge of the heroism of their unknown Hindu colleague, whose name ought to hold its place on the roll of those who have fallen in a noble fight, and whose very death marks a victory. Though she had so painfully striven to preserve her caste in a foreign land, it seemed doubtful at first whether the Brâhmans of Poonah would receive her as pure, after her long sojourn among unbelievers. But humanity proved too strong even for caste. Men and women, old and young, orthodox and unorthodox, all received the young Doctor with open arms, paid her friendly visits, and extended to her a most cordial welcome. Her own friends were astonished at the unprecedented concession made in her favour by the strictly orthodox party. And when the end came the whole of Poonah seemed to share in the mourning of the family, and the fear that the priests might raise objections to cremating her body according to the sacred rites of the Hindus, proved perfectly groundless. Not only on the occasion of her funeral, but earlier, when her husband offered sacrifices to the gods and the guardian planets to avert their anger and her death, the priests showed no sign of any prejudice against him or her. This, too, is a victory, for it shows that even the most inveterate social and religious diseases are not incurable when treated with unselfish love and generosity. If all this could be achieved by a frail young daughter of India, what is there that could be called impossible for the strong men of that country? Even now her example has been followed, and Ânandibâi's life has not been in vain.

NATIONAL CHARACTER OF THE HINDUS.

No wonder that those who look upon the Indian nation as an inferior race should have so often protested against my judgment of them as prejudiced and as far too favourable. I know quite well that the men and women of whom I have here spoken are exceptional beings. They would be exceptional in England also, and anywhere else. But exceptions, after all, represent possibilities, and the good work achieved by such men as Rammohun Roy, Keshub Chunder Sen, and Malabâri, or by Râmabâi, shows how much of real power lies dormant in the people of India. If it is always wise in judging of people to look more to their strong than to their weak points; why should we, in trying to determine the average intellectual and moral stature of the Hindus, take account of their dwarfs rather than of their giants? Is it right, for instance, to say that all Indians are liars? It is a very hackneyed charge, but it is never forgotten, and it often crops up again when least expected. Because culprits before an Indian judge and witnesses before a jury, nay, even cooks and butlers in Anglo-Indian homes have occasionally, or even frequently, told lies, does it follow that all Indians are liars? It is unfortunate that so many who have spent their lives as civil servants or officers in India should represent the few hundreds or the few thousands of people with whom they have been brought into contact at Calcutta, Benares, Bombay, or Madras as fair specimens of the people of India at large. It should never be forgotten that the true home of the Indians is in their villages, and that those who go to Calcutta or other great towns to take service in English families are by no means the best specimens of the Indian population. They are willing to submit for some time to the unkind treatment which they not seldom receive from men, women, and children of alien origin; but they can but seldom feel any real attachment or even respect for their employers, though here, too, there are most honourable exceptions. From the earliest times truthfulness has always been mentioned as a national characteristic of the inhabitants of India, and we are now told that all Indians are liars! We cannot open any of the ancient law-books or epic poems without coming across such sentences as "Truth is the ladder to heaven and the ship across the ocean"; "The end of all the Vedas is Truth"; "Seeking after all the virtues, I have nowhere found anything so purifying as Truth." We appeal to the literatures of other nations as records of their true character, why not in the case of the Hindus? It is easy to say that all this is changed now, and that those who have been magistrates and judges in India ought to know best. But do these judges consider the peculiar difficulties with which the lower classes in India have to contend, being ruled by men of a different colour, of a different language, and a different religion? Would they expect or find much regard for truth even in an English sailor if examined by a French, ay, even by an English judge? It is easy to be truthful if you have nothing to fear, but we must not wonder if, to escape an oath or a kick, a native servant will now and then tell a lie to his master. Anyhow, one case, a hundred, nay, a thousand cases are not sufficient to condemn a whole nation of more than two hundred millions. It has been my rule through life never to accept any of these sweeping assertions about a whole nation. If I hear a man calling all Indians liars, I generally ask how many he has known, and I do the same when I hear all Frenchmen called monkeys, all Italians assassins, all Germans unwashed, all Russians savages, or even England *Perfide Albion*. I have never in all my life repented having had eyes for the bright side rather than the dark side of nations as well as of individuals. I hoped I had exposed the fallacy and folly of such undiscriminating accusations in the Lectures which I gave at Cambridge, to the candidates for the Indian Civil Service, Lect. 2, "On the Truthful Character of the Hindus." But no, the old charge is brought up again and again. That some members of the Indian Civil Service who had for years to deal with native servants and tradesmen should have had some painful experiences, who can doubt? Even within the small circle of my own personal acquaintances I have met with Indians who disregarded the old commandment of telling the truth; but to generalise in such matters, from a limited number of instances, is surely against all the rules of inductive logic. This prejudice against the inhabitants of India as being a nation of liars may become really dangerous in its consequences. Even now, as the press is open to the ruled as well as to the rulers of India, the charge of ingrained untruthfulness has been hurled back most savagely by the accused on the accusers. It always is so, and there is in the end but one remedy, even when an inclination towards untruthfulness does exist, and that is trust. I have no doubt that I shall be much abused again for having ventured to say so much, and to stand up for the people of India, and particularly for having produced evidence in support of my opinion, taken from their literature, ancient and modern, from their sacred books, their law-books, and their philosophical systems. Such evidence is admitted when we judge of any other nation; why should it be ruled out of court in the case of the people of India?

Missionaries seem to imagine that they have a better chance of spreading their own religion by vilifying the popular religion of India, and trying to show that all the vices of the people are due to it. King Asoka, in the third century B.C., knew better, when he had his edicts engraved all over his kingdom, and declared "that people should never praise their own religion or disparage other religions without a cause; and that whenever there is a cause, our words should be moderate." Our own missionaries might safely take these words to heart. At all events, no virtue stands higher in the eyes of the founders of the Indian religion than truthfulness, and if religion has any influence in forming the character of a whole nation, no nation should be more truthful than that of India.

I am far from being an indiscriminate admirer of India, and, if I am told that I exaggerate the good qualities of the people, I am quite willing to confess that even among the small number of young men who are now sent every year from India to England, and particularly to Oxford, I have myself had some disappointing experiences. Want of straightforwardness arising from want of moral courage, want of truthfulness arising from a desire to please, hollow pretence amounting in some cases to actual deception, all these I have witnessed among the young men who now come to spend two or three years at Oxford. But may we not look upon these defects as clouds that will pass? And are there never any cases of untruthfulness when there has been a disturbance in college, or when an election has to be carried, *coûte qu' il coûte.* The worst of it is that those who complain of untruthfulness in others, cannot help posing as patterns of truthfulness themselves.

I may mention some curious cases. A young Bengali told me that he came all the way from Benares to Oxford, because he had been told by his friends who had contributed money towards the founding of an Indian Institute there, that he would be received there and enabled to attend lectures in the University. How he had paid his passage money I cannot understand, but I believe the poor boy was actually starving when he came to me, and he was in despair, when I had to tell him that there was no such institution at Oxford, and no scholarships open to him as he had been led to imagine. He told me that he had been to the Indian Institute, but could get no help. He told me that he saw no students or teachers there, but only stuffed animals. "My friends in India," he said, "have been asked to subscribe money for the benefit of Indian students at Oxford, but no one would even speak to me or help me there. If one of your students," he added, "came to Benares, our Pandits would receive him with open arms, teach him all they know, and gladly give him food and lodging." "Yes," I said, "but the laws of Manu do not apply to England." I gave him the little he wanted, but what became of him afterwards I cannot tell, nor how he found the means of returning to his own country. I confess I was at first a little suspicious, but, after all, his story may have been true, and what then?

The manners of the young Indians when they arrive at Oxford are generally excellent, but they soon acquire what they consider English manners, rough and ready, bluff and blunt, and by no means an improvement on their own. The same young man who at first enters your room with folded hands and a graceful salám, will after a very short time walk in, sit down, stretch out his legs, and address you in the most familiar terms. They imagine that this is English. Some profess to know Sanskrit, and pour out a stream of words which at school they may have learnt by heart, but often with an utter disregard of case and gender. Some who had failed, as we afterwards were informed by the authorities, to even pass their matriculation examination in Sanskrit at the Calcutta University, posed as Pandits at Oxford, expressing at the same time their undisguised contempt for all who professed to know and to teach Sanskrit in the Universities of England. These men have a very curious way of blushing. If you convict them of a downright falsehood, their bright brown colour turns suddenly greyish, but their eloquence in defending themselves never fades or flags.

Altogether the experiment of sending young Hindus to prepare for the Civil Service Examination in England has not, as far as I have been able to judge, proved a great success. At Oxford they find it very hard to make friends among the better class of undergraduates. Most of our undergraduates come from public schools, and have plenty of friends of their own. If they are asked to be kind to any of the Indian students, all they can do, or really be expected to do, is to invite them once or twice to a breakfast party. They have hardly any interests in common with them, and anything like friendship is out of the question. If the young students from India have money to spend, there is danger of their falling into bad company, and even if they pass their examinations, I am afraid that some of them return to India not much improved by their English exile. The worst of it is that they often return *désillusionné.* At first everything English is grand and perfect in their eyes, an Oxford degree is the highest goal of their ambition. But when they have obtained it, chiefly by learning by heart, they make very light of it. And this making light of it is soon applied to other things English also, which they hear constantly criticised or abused, particularly in the newspapers and in Parliament, so that they often leave England better informed, it may be, but hardly better affected towards the Government which they are meant to serve. The present state of things is certainly discouraging, particularly as it seems impossible to suggest any real remedy. But here also there are bright exceptions, and I have always held that we must judge of things by their bright rather than by their dark sides. There are, and there always will be, difficulties in the intercourse between Europeans and Orientals. It is wonderful to see how well they have been overcome in the Government of India. Natives in the Civil Service or at the Bar seem to work quite harmoniously with their English colleagues, and even after they have reached high employment, and have to exercise authority, little has been heard of conflicts, whether caused by arrogance or subserviency. There are Continental statesmen who, while they cannot help admiring the English system of governing India, look upon it as suicidal in the end. They consider the Russian system of complete repression as the only right system of dealing with Orientals, and as far more merciful in the end. Well, we must wait for the end; but, whatever it may be, it seems right to treat the inhabitants of India as they have been hitherto treated by the Government and by the wisest rulers of India, not as born enemies or as conspirators to be kept under by force, but as loyal subjects to be trusted. Of course, there sometimes will be troubles, for how can it be expected that in two or three hundred millions of conquered subjects there should be no grumbling, no disaffection, no fanaticism? The government of India by a mere handful of Englishmen is, indeed, an achievement unparalleled in the whole history of the world. The suppression of the Indian mutiny shows what stuff English soldiers and statesmen are made of. If people say that ours is not an age for Epic poetry, let them read Lord Roberts' "Forty-one Years in India." When I see in a circus a man standing with outstretched legs on two or three horses, and two men standing on his shoulders, and other men standing on theirs, and a little child at the top of all, while the horses are running full gallop round the arena, I feel what I feel when watching the government of India. One hardly dares to breathe, and one wishes one could persuade one's neighbours also to sit still and hold their breath. If ever there were an accident, the crash would be fearful, and who would suffer most? Fortunately, by this time the people of India know all this, and they have learnt to appreciate what they owe not only to the *Pax*, but to the *Lux Britannica*. If one could dare to read the mind of three hundred millions, I should say that in the present state of things the people of India, as a whole, want no change except such changes as can be achieved by ordinary constitutional means. It is true that I have not known a large number of Indians, but I have known Indians who could well speak in the name of large numbers, and they speak to me more openly perhaps than to others, looking upon me as a kind of Mle*kkh*a, but at the same time as half an Indian. Some young Indian Râjahs while travelling in Switzerland, found themselves lately in the same railway carriage with some Russian princes and noblemen. They had been discussing among themselves some of their grievances in English, and the Russians, who of course understood English, after listening to them for some time, became very communicative, and began to explain to them the beneficent rule of the Tsar. They even went so far as to hold out a hope to them of an Indian Parliament, as soon as the Russians were settled in Calcutta. On parting they asked the Indian princes, "When shall we see you at St. Petersburg?" And they were not a little taken aback when the strangers bowed and smiled, and said, "We are going just now to be present at the opening of Parliament in London. We should like very much to see St. Petersburg afterwards, and to be present at the opening of your Parliament there. . . ."

Again and again have I been urged to go to India, and have been told many a time by people who had spent a few months there that I could never hope to know the Indians, to understand Indian literature, or even pronounce Sanskrit properly without having passed a vacation at Calcutta or Bombay. I would have given anything to go to India when I was young. There was a time when I was on the point of becoming a missionary in order to be able to spend some years in India. But what a strange missionary I should have made! What I cared to know in India were not the Râjahs and Mahârâjahs, the streets of Bombay, the towers of silence, or the temples of Ellora. What I cared to see were the few remaining *S*rotriyas who still knew their Vedas by heart, who would have talked to me and shaken hands with me, even though I was a Mle*kkh*a. Had they not asked me even at a distance to act as one of the sixteen priests at their Shrâddhs (*S*râddhas), their funeral services? Had they not asked me to recite Vedic prayers for the souls of their deceased fathers? Had they not actually sent me the same presents which on those occasions they are bound to give to their priests, because, as they wrote, I knew the Veda better than their own priests? Had they not actually sent me the sacred Brahmanic thread which I am as proud to wear as any more brilliant decoration?

Here is a letter which I received some years ago beautifully printed in gold:—

> RESPECTED SIR,—On the occasion of my departed father's Shraddh ceremony, which was celebrated some months ago, amongst the offerings to Adhyâpaks and Âchâryas (teachers), an offering was made to you in consideration of your eminent services to the laws of Sanskrit literature (*sic*). I am a believer in the New Dispensation of the Brahmo-Somâj of India, which teaches reverence to the great and good men of all lands and religions. I trust you will kindly accept the piece of shawl sent in separate parcels, and pronounce your blessing both for me and for the spirit of my honoured father in heaven.

Was it very wrong or sacrilegious that I did so? I extract a few sentences from the letter I wrote in reply:—

> I deeply sympathise with your Shrâddh ceremony; nay, I wish we had something like it in our own religion. To keep alive the memory of our parents, to feel their presence during the great trials of our life, to be influenced by what we know they would have wished us to do, and to

try to honour their name by showing ourselves not unworthy bearers of it, that is a Shrâddh ceremony in which we can all partake, nay, ought to partake, whatever our religion may be. There is a real, though unseen bond of union (tantu) that connects us through our parents and ancestors with the Great Author of all things, and the same bond will connect ourselves through our children with the most distant generations. If we know that, and are constantly reminded of it by ceremonies like that of your Shrâddh, we are not likely to forget the responsibility that rests on every one of us. In that sense your Shrâddh is a blessing, on your parents because on yourselves, and whatever the future of your religion may be in India, I hope this communion with the spirits of your ancestors, or Pitris, will always form an essential part of it.

Two or three years in India would certainly have been a delight to me, but short of that I did not care to go. I was quite satisfied with that ideal India which I had built up for myself, whether from their books or from those who had come to see me at Oxford. If my India, as I am often told, is an ideal India, is it more so than Greece as seen through the poems of Homer, or Italy as seen through the verses of Virgil? What is ideal is not necessarily unreal, it is only like a landscape seen in sunshine. Look at a landscape on a brilliant summer's day bathed in light and verdure, and again on a bleak day of March with its bitter winds and cloudy sky. It is the same landscape, but which of the two is its true aspect? I shall not speak here of ancient Indian poets, of ancient Indian philosophers, or of ancient Indian heroes. What I feel, and what I wish my friends would feel with me, is that a country which, even in these unheroic days, could produce a Rammohun Roy, a Keshub Chunder Sen, a Malabâri, and a Râmabâi, is not a decadent country, but may look forward to a bright, sunny future, as it can look back with satisfaction and even pride on four thousand years of a not inglorious history.

I have never bestowed excessive praise on Indian literature, nor do I feel answerable for having filled the brains of native scholars with exaggerated ideas about its value. Its value to us is great, but chiefly from a historical point of view, and this is just what native scholars find it so difficult to understand. No wonder that after Goethe had bestowed such superlative praise on the Sanskrit play of "*S*akuntalâ," the Hindus should have spoken of their Kâlidâsa as the equal of Shakespeare. They forget that what surprised Goethe was not only the beauty of Kâlidâsa's poetry, great as it is, but its antiquity, and the fact that such refined poetry should have existed where it was least expected, and at a time when it could not have been matched by the poetry of any other country.

INDIAN THEOSOPHY.

Empty panegyrics are always to be deprecated, and I am afraid that great and lasting mischief has been wrought, for instance, by Madame Blavatsky and her friends who went to India, ignorant of Sanskrit and Sanskrit literature, and who have for years been proclaiming to the world at large that Hindu philosophy, particularly that of the Vedânta and that of Buddhism, which they did not always distinguish very carefully one from the other, was infinitely superior to all the philosophies of Europe, that the Brâhmans even at the present day were the depositories of the primeval wisdom of the world, and that by the united efforts of Madame Blavatsky and Dayânanda Sarasvati a new theosophy would dawn on India and Europe which would eclipse all former systems of thought. Poor Dayânanda Sarasvati had no idea of what Madame Blavatsky was thinking of; but, though bewildered for a time by the unaccustomed adulation poured on him and the extravagant veneration paid to him by Europeans, he soon recovered, and declined to have anything to do with the Polish prophetess and her vagaries.

Mme. Blavatsky might certainly have done a good work if she had joined some really learned Pandits, familiar with the six systems of Hindu philosophy; nor would it have been too much for a person endowed with such extraordinary, if not miraculous, powers as she was said to have possessed, to have mastered the grammar of Sanskrit. But what has been the result of all her labours? Indian philosophy has gained some Corybantic followers, but the true teaching of Bâdarâya*n*a and Kapila has been obscured rather than illuminated by being mixed up with poor and contemptible conjuring tricks. New prejudices have been roused against the noble philosophies of Vedânta, Sâ*m*khya, and Yoga which it will take many years to remove. Why not take the authoritative texts of these systems, many of which have been translated into English and German, and place their essential doctrines in a clear and intelligible form before the philosophic public of Europe? There is no mystery about that philosophy, or about the Mahâtmans who are versed in it. There is nothing esoteric in their teaching; all is open to those who are properly qualified and trustworthy. Their Upanishads and Dar*s*anas can be studied exactly like the philosophies of Plato or Des Cartes—nay, even better, because every one of their tenets has been put down in their Sûtras very clearly and definitely by Indian philosophers far more so than by Plato or Hegel. It is difficult, therefore, not to get angry if one sees the elevated views of these ancient philosophers dragged down to the level of cloudy hallucinations, and rendered absurd by being mixed up with vulgar trickeries. "Corruptio optimi pessima."

I have often been blamed for the hard judgments which I have pronounced against Madame Blavatsky and her friends. I have been told that she and her friends have done good by rousing a new interest in their ancient philosophy among the people of India, and by attracting the attention of European thinkers towards it. If that is so, let it be to their credit; but I feel convinced that no good has ever come from anything that is not perfectly honest and straightforward; and what a lurid light has been thrown on the Theosophist Society at Adyar! There is no excuse for such things, however good the intention may have been, and even now, when I see well-intentioned men like Vivekânanda preaching the doctrines of the Upanishads, of Bâdarâya*n*a and *S*a*m*kara in America, and gaining, as I read, numerous converts, I still seem to perceive now and then something of the old Blavatsky leaven that has not yet been entirely thrown off. Vedântism requires no bush, no trappings, no tricks. What we want is a historical and critical treatment, just the same as that which has been applied to Plato and Aristotle.

When I saw hundreds of people running after Madame Blavatsky and her apostles, and the texts and the excellent translations of the philosophical Sûtras hardly looked at, an old Oriental story often came into my mind. The story is a mere illustration, a D*ri*sh*t*ânta, but it is full of truth.

"A certain man had the peculiar power of grunting exactly like a pig, so much so that whenever he grunted where pigs were grazing they would all turn round to see if any new member had come into their fold. This man's fame spread abroad, and he began a tour to obtain money by means of his art. Wherever he went he erected a pandal, and issued tickets for admission, all of which got exhausted very soon, such was the eagerness of people to hear him grunt. While he was thus making money in a village a sage happened to pass by with his disciples, and it struck him that he could teach a good lesson to them through this incident. Accordingly he ordered a small pandal to be erected, and advertised that even better grunting would be heard here than in the other pandal, and that free of cost. The people were naturally very eager to hear it, and they visited it. The sage brought a real pig before them, and squeezing it a little, made it grunt. Really the grunt was much better than the man's, but the people exclaimed, 'Pooh, is this all? We hear this every day, but what is there in it? It is nothing wonderful,' and went away. The sage said, 'Here is a splendid lesson for us. We seldom care for reality, but always go in for imitation.' That is why even this world exists, which is a mere imitation, a reflection in the distorting mirror of Mâyâ, of the great Âtman. No external help is required to see the Self, but very few care for it, and, even if you eagerly advertise it, none will go to you except those who love truth for truth's sake. Reflect on this."

This story is a mere parable, and, as such, cannot possibly offend anybody. At all events, if anybody might complain, it would be the showman of the real pig, not the mere imitator. I have never seen Madame Blavatsky. She threatened once she would come to Oxford to face and to confound me, but she never did. Though she preached to the undergraduates at Balliol, she never came near me. It is simply my love of genuine Indian philosophy that induced me to protest against what I knew to be a mere travesty of Vedânta, Sâ*m*khya, and Yoga philosophy. If even in this travestied form Indian philosophy has found friends, in India and Europe, owing to her preaching, I am quite content, but Satyam paramo dharma*h*, "Truth is the highest religion," or the highest virtue, and nothing, I am deeply convinced, can prosper for any length of time that is mixed up with exaggeration or untruth. If it is right and our bounden duty to protest against foolish disfigurements of our own religion, why should misrepresentation of the Hindu religion and Hindu philosophy be allowed to pass unchallenged?

From what I have seen and read of Vivekânanda and his colleagues, they seem to me honestly bent on doing good work, and I feel the same about the propaganda carried on by Dharmapâla in favour of Buddhism. It is honest, it is unselfish, it is free from juggling. Vivekânanda and the other followers of Râmak*ri*sh*n*a ought, however, to teach their followers how to distinguish between the perfervid utterances of their teacher, Râmak*ri*sh*n*a, an enthusiastic Bhakta (devotee), and the clear and dry style of the Sûtras of Bâdarâya*n*a. The Vedânta spirit is there, but the form often becomes too vague and exaggerated to give us an idea of what the true *Gn*ânin (knower) ought to be. However, as long as these devoted preachers keep true to the Upanishads, the Sûtras, and the recognised commentaries, whether of *S*a*m*kara or of Râmânu*g*a, I wish them all the success which they deserve by their unselfish devotion and their high ideals.

MY INDIAN CORRESPONDENTS.

Were I to publish any of the innumerable letters which I receive from unknown correspondents from every part of India, some written in English, others in Sanskrit, they would surprise many readers by showing how like the present political, philosophic, and religious atmosphere in the higher classes of Indian society is to our own. My Indian friends are interested in the same questions which interest us, and they often refer us to their own ancient philosophers who have discussed the same questions many centuries ago. Many of them read and write English perfectly well, though there is a certain bluntness in their questions which would startle us in England.

While I am writing these lines, a letter signed by a number of Indian gentlemen is lying on my table, as yet unanswered, and, if the nature of the questions be considered, likely to remain unanswered for some time. To us some of these questions sound certainly very startling, but they are nevertheless interesting, because they show us the problems on which the Indian mind is brooding, and which to many of them are like their daily bread. We ourselves are more inclined to suppress questions of this kind, or to say with Sir Philip Sidney, "Reason cannot show itself more reasonable than to leave off reasoning on things above reason." To Indian thinkers, however, there seem to be no regions at all which cannot be approached and penetrated by human reason.

The questions on which my unknown friends want my answer, and probably expect it by return of post, are :—

(1) What is your opinion regarding God and soul? Is the latter a reflection of the former, or is the one quite separate from the other?

Athanasius might have answered such a question, but how can I?

(2) If both God and soul are said to have been separated from the beginning, then how, when, and whence is the latter afflicted with Karman (acts and their results) which cause sad suffering to each individual soul?

(3) Is the universe eternal and self-abiding, or has it been created by some one?

(4 A) Taking it for granted that there is some one to be considered the Creator of the universe, we want to know what was the period of the creation, and how long the creation will last; what it was at first, and what will it be hereafter? Did the Creator create all beings (old and young, children and parents) in a moment, or did He create them in succession? Were male and female created at the same time, or one after the other?

(4 B) Did the Creator bestow rewards on the actions of men in a former life, or did He create them freely of His own accord? Is He the Giver of rewards, the Ruler of the Universe, or simply the Creator?

(4 C) How is it, then, that God created rich and poor, happy and sad? What were the acts that could have produced such results?

(5) What is the real matter of the five elements —earth, water, fire, air, and ether, and of the soul? What is the origin of the smallest atoms (paramâ*n*u) and of time?

(6) Is there any method which, acted upon, will save us from anxieties and troubles of this world, and by means of which we may reach Nirvâ*n*a?

(7) What was the origin of idol worship? Is it good, or is it contrary to the Sacred Books?

(8) Was Buddhism an offshoot of *G*ainism, or vice versa? or have both religions arisen separately from time immemorial?

(9) By whom were the Vedas compiled, and what do they treat of?

(10) Where does the soul go to after death? Is there any heaven or hell in which the rewards of actions, both good and bad, are to be enjoyed?

My correspondents, who are evidently men of cultivated minds, describe themselves simply as cloth-merchants. I know nothing more about them, but we may learn from their letter what is the unseen stream of thought running through India. They seem to belong to the Digambara sect of the *G*ain religion. I doubt whether any English cloth-merchants would have appealed to J. S. Mill or to Darwin for a solution of such metaphysical difficulties. We may consider such questions unreasonable, only we must not imagine that because we do not speak of these riddles, we ourselves have solved them. Nay, it may be useful to be reminded from time to time of the limits of our knowledge, so as not to trust too much to the omniscience of our own philosophers.

I often feel ashamed that I cannot answer such letters. But first of all, let me assure my kind correspondents that I am not omniscient, and never pretended to be so. On some of the questions they ask me, their own philosophers have said all that can be said, more even than our own. But let them consider likewise that with the best will on my part, I should have no time left for my own studies, were I to attempt to enter on a discussion of such problems as are set before me by my unknown friends in India and elsewhere. Every one who writes to me seems to imagine that he is the only person who does so. If they saw the chaos of unanswered letters on my table they would see that I do not exaggerate, and would understand that it would be physically impossible for any human being to answer all the letters addressed to me. Life has its limits, every day has its limits, and one hour out of the twenty-four might well be left to an old man for dreaming, for looking back on the years and the friends that are gone, and forward to that life to which our stay on earth forms, as he thinks, but a short prelude.

In one respect, as I pointed out before, the Indians differ from us very characteristically. They give very free expression to their sentiments, whether of love or of admiration, and even when they have to express their disapproval they do it in the gentlest and least offensive words. Some of them have expressed to me on several occasions their surprise, nay, disgust, at the rudeness and coarseness of certain Sanskrit scholars in their literary controversies. Some people may call Oriental gentleness and courtesy flattery, some dishonesty, and it certainly would be so for us. Even in French and Italian, however, there are some expressions which we would not use in English, and which, if translated into English, sound to us unreal and exaggerated, while not to use them would amount in French to a want of politeness. We are not so easily *enchanted* or *ravished*, nor are we always *devoted servants*, but at the same time I must confess that our *yours truly* sounds almost brutal in answer to the eloquent finish of the letters of our French friends. But though I fully admit that considerable deductions must be made from the panegyrics addressed to us by our Indian correspondents, it would be wrong to accuse them of intentional insincerity. If their panegyrics seem sometimes to come very near to an apotheosis, we must not forget that their Devas or gods are not looked upon as anything very extraordinary after all.

I must mention at least one instance when I was agreeably surprised by the thorough sincerity of one of my Indian correspondents, who certainly meant far more than he said. The Mahârâjah of Vizianagram wrote to me some years ago expressing a wish to possess a copy of my edition of the "Rig-Veda" in six volumes. It had been published at £15, but when I applied to a second-hand bookseller he charged £24, and told me that complete copies of the book were getting very scarce. Soon after the Mahârâjah wrote again asking the bookseller to send him a second copy, but he was informed by his agent in England that he could not get a complete set for love or for money. The Mahârâjah wrote to ask me why I did not bring out a new edition, and I had to tell him what the expense of printing such a work would be, and that, though I should gladly give my labour for nothing,

I could not find a publisher in England, not even a University Press, to undertake such a work. The Indian Government had for years used the first edition for making presents in Europe and in India, and though in this way it had fully reimbursed itself for the original outlay, it was not inclined to venture on a second edition. Upon this the Mahârâjah, who had hitherto been most lavish in his praises of the work, showed that the praise he had bestowed on it was not mere empty praise, but was really meant. After telling me what his Pandits had said to him, and sending me some valuable MSS., as a present, which they had prepared for me, he offered to pay himself for the printing of a new edition, if I would undertake the labour of revising the text.

This I readily accepted, and in two years, 1890 to 1892, a new, and I hope more correct edition, was issued from the Press at Oxford in four large volumes. The Mahârâjah paid to the Press not less than £4,000. I found out afterwards that this Indian nobleman was by no means a student, an antiquarian, or a theologian; but, on the contrary, a man of the world, very fond of racing and hunting. He distinguished himself on one occasion, as I was told, by riding up the staircase to the very roof of his palace. When in one of my last letters I asked him what had induced him to spend so large a sum on the Rig-Veda, he replied that India wanted its Bible, and he added, "It may benefit me hereafter." That hereafter has come sooner than he expected. He died a comparatively young man, and as long as the Veda lives his name will certainly not be forgotten. The Veda has lived now for four thousand years, or, according to Indian ideas, it has existed from all eternity. Four thousand years is but a small slice of eternity, but are there many books that have lasted or will last four thousand years? I ought to add that his liberality did not stop at paying the expenses of the work, but that he placed a large number of copies at my disposal, which was more than I expected or deserved. Are there many Mahârâjahs or Zemindârs in Europe who would have spent so large a sum on a new edition of the Bible, or, in fact, of any other important book? Would any scholar even think of appealing to the millionaires of England or America to help him in bringing out an old forgotten book, if it "benefitted them hereafter" only? Anyhow, I came to learn that Hindus are not simply grandiloquent, but that they can do grand things also, when the opportunity offers.

If I finish here the list of my Indian friends, it is not because I have no more names to add. We have lately had a book called "Representative Indians," by C. P. Pillai, 1897, containing biographical sketches of thirty-six distinguished Hindus and Parsis. Many of them I have known or corresponded with, but of their sentiments, their hopes and disappointments, I know but little. The undercurrent of their life, the deeper motives of their actions, are under a kind of purdah, and we hardly ever get either autobiographical confessions or outspoken memoirs. This is a pity, and naturally deprives reminiscences of Indian friends of much of that human interest which everybody feels when catching glimpses of the more intimate life of distinguished persons. We seldom hear of a good or smart saying from a Hindu, such as we have in large numbers from English, German, or French statesmen or poets. The people of India are still a deep secret to us, and if I have succeeded in withdrawing the curtain from only a small portion of their inmost thoughts and feelings, if, here and there, I have helped to change mere curiosity about them into a warm human sympathy with them, my reminiscences will have fulfilled their true object. In some respects, and particularly in respect to the greatest things (*τὰ μέγιστα*), India has as much to teach us as Greece and Rome, nay, I should say more. We must not forget, of course, that we are the direct intellectual heirs of the Greeks, and that our philosophical currency is taken from the capital left to us by them. Our palates are accustomed to the food which they have supplied to us from our very childhood, and hence whatever comes to us now from the thought-mines of India is generally put aside as merely curious or strange, whether in language, mythology, religion, or philosophy. But however foreign Indian thought may appear to us, it has filled an important place in the growth of the human race, and that growth is important, whether it took place on the borders of the Ilissos or on the shores of the Ganges. In India we still see, as it were, the last traces of the primordial surprise at this world. Their earliest thinkers seem still to feel strange in it, while Greeks and Romans are thoroughly at home in their little world. No doubt the Greeks as well as the Indians saw the riddles of the world, were perplexed by them, and tried to solve them. But while Greeks and Romans, and later on the leading races of Europe also, settled down to their practical work in life, the Indians, at least the leading thinkers among them, never felt quite at ease even in their beautiful forests, by the side of their mighty rivers, or under the shadow of their gigantic snow-mountains in the north. They never cared so intensely for this span of life on earth as the Greeks did. Hence they never brought political life to its full development, like the Greeks and Romans; they never strove to conquer what was not theirs, or to govern the world which they had conquered; nor did they, like the Hebrews, look upon the exact fulfilment of the law as the highest object of our life on earth. Even while passing through this world, their eyes were for ever fixed on the Beyond. They strove to pierce through the dark roof of their forests, to travel to the distant sources of their rivers, and to transcend even the snowy peaks of the Himâlaya Mountains. Their hearts would never forget the life that lay behind them, and their minds were for ever set on the life that was to come.

The old questions of Whence? Why? and Whither? fascinated and enthralled their thoughts. They may have but little of practical wisdom to teach us, for they paid but small attention to the arts of peace and war. But, though they fell in consequence an easy prey to their neighbours, they had something nevertheless which their barbarous conquerors had not. They had their own view of the world, and this view, different as it is from our own, deserves to be looked at carefully and seriously by us. Whatever we may think of the world which they had built up for themselves, and in which they lived, their idea of the Godhead is certainly higher, purer, and more consistent than that of Greeks,

Romans, and Hebrews. They passed through polytheism, henotheism, and monotheism, and they arrived at last at what is generally called pantheism, but a pantheism very different from vulgar pantheism. They started with the firm conviction that what we mean by God must be a Being without a second, without beginning or end, without limitations of any kind. Whatever there is or seems to be, call it mind or matter, man or nature, can have one substance only, one and the same, whatever we name it, God, or Brahman, the Absolute, or the Supreme Being. They never say, like other pantheists, that everything in this phenomenal world is God, but that everything has its being in God.

How the change from the real to the phenomenal came about, or, as we say, how the world was created, they can tell us as little as we can tell them. They simply point to the fact that it has come about, that it is there, that it is and can be nothing but phenomenal to us, but that the phenomenal could not even seem to be without the real behind it. In order to restore the phenomenal world to its reality, they hold that all that is wanted is knowledge or philosophy, which destroys that universal Nescience which makes us all take the phenomenal for the real, the objective for the subjective. Their philosophy is chiefly the

Vedânta, though other systems also pursue the same object. Each man is in substance or in self identical with God, for what else could he be? If they say that each man is God, that would, no doubt, offend us, but that man and everything else has its true being in the Godhead is a very different kind of pantheism. To regain that full self-consciousness or God-consciousness, to return to God, to break down the artificial wall that seemed to separate man from God, is the highest object of Indian philosophy, and in some form or other these thoughts have gradually leavened all classes of society from the highest to the lowest.

In order to be able to appreciate the true value of the Vedânta, we have to study its growth in the Upanishads, and in the minute disquisitions of the Vedânta-Sûtras and their commentaries. No doubt these are sometimes very tedious, and to us, in this age of the world, may often appear childish and useless. And yet the Vedânta view of the world has a right to claim the same attention as that of Heraclitus, Plato, Spinoza, or Kant. It is as true and as untrue as any of these philosophical intuitions, but it possesses an attraction of its own which has held the best minds of India captive for generations, and will continue to do so for ages to come.

Nay, as we have always had among us Platonists, Spinozists, and Kantians, the time will come, nay, has come already, when European philosophers will try to look at the world through the glasses of the Vedânta also. It is well known that Schopenhauer, no mean thinker of modern times, declared the Vedânta as taught in the Upanishads "the product of the highest wisdom" (*Ausgeburt der höchsten Weisheit*). May not these words make other philosophers pause before they reject as childish a philosophy which Schopenhauer placed above the philosophy of Giordano Bruno, Malebranche, and Spinoza?

India should be known, not from without, but from within, and it will require a long time and far abler hands than mine before we really know what India was meant to be in the development of mankind. Heinrich Simon remarked very truly, "Our history is miserable because we have no biographies. . . . If a man's life lies open before me from day to day in all his acts and all his thoughts, so far as they can be represented externally, I gain a better insight into the history of the time than by the best general representation of it." What we want to know is, how the prominent men of India imbibed the Vedânta, and how the principles they had imbibed from that source influenced their lives, their acts, and their thoughts. With us philosophy remains always something collateral only. Our mainstay is formed by religion and ethics. But with the Hindus, philosophy is life in full earnest, it is but another name for religion, while morality has a place assigned to it as an essential preliminary to all philosophy. Most of our greatest philosophers and of their followers seem to lead two lives, one as it ought to be, the other as it is. One of our greatest philosophers, Berkeley, knew quite well what the world is, but he lived as a bishop, unconcerned about the unreal character of all with which he had to deal. There have been cases of true Vedântists, also, who have led useful, active lives as ministers and organisers of states, but he who has grasped the highest truths of the Vedânta, or has been grasped by them, is driven at once into the solitude of the forests, waiting there for the solution of all riddles, for perfect freedom, and in the end for the truest freedom of all, for death—*Θανοῦμαι καὶ ἐλευθερήσομαι.*

MY INDIAN FRIENDS

IV

THE VEDA

We live no longer in times when the head of a great publishing firm would ask a scholar who offered a translation of the Veda, as I know the late Professor H. H. Wilson was asked, "But what in all the world is the Veda, or what you call the Rig-Veda?" But nevertheless in spite of the years that have passed since, I am still asked from time to time much the same question, and I confess I cannot answer it in two words.

I should not be surprised if even some of those who are doing me the honour of reading my Recollections of Auld Lang Syne, and who in this volume of recollections of my Indian Friends, have so often come across the name of Veda, were to say in their secret heart, What in all the world can that Veda be to which this misguided man has devoted the whole of his life? I have been asked such a question before now, and it is perhaps not unreasonable that I should try to answer it here. For after all, was not the Veda the first of my Indian friends? Was it not the bridge that led me from West to East, from Greece and Italy to India, nay, from Dessau to Oxford, from Germany to England? Whatever other people may say about the misguided man who sacrificed everything to the Veda, I still count the Veda among my best friends, and I sometimes regret that my duties as Professor of Comparative Philology in the University of Oxford should during my later years have withdrawn my full allegiance from it. What then is the Veda?

The Vedas, as we possess them, are four systematically arranged collections of hymns and verses, and the Veda is often used in the sense of these four Vedas taken together. The first and most important Veda is the Rig-Veda, which has often, and not without some truth, been called the only true Veda. It contains 1017, or with some additions, the Vâlakkhilya-hymns, 1028 hymns, each on an average containing about ten verses. They are all addressed to Devatâs or deities, and whatever subject is addressed in these hymns, down to bows, arrows, and stones, is supposed to become, *ipso facto*, a Devatâ, while the poet is called the seer or Rishi. The metres are numerous and strictly regulated, though there is more freedom in them than in the later artificial poetry of India.

The hymns of the Rig-Veda were meant to be recited at sacrifices, and this is no doubt the explanation of their careful preservation during many centuries, by means of a strictly regulated oral tradition.

The second, the Sâma-Veda is a much smaller collection of hymns, most of them borrowed from the Rig-Veda, but different in character so far as they were meant to be sung at the ancient sacrifices.

The third, the Ya*g*ur-Veda, consists of sacrificial formulas and of verses to be repeated in a low voice by a class of priests who were entrusted chiefly with the manual work required for the performance of sacrifices.

The fourth, the Atharva-Veda, probably collected at a later time, contains, besides many hymns from the Rig-Veda, a large number of popular verses used for magical and medicinal purposes, some of them possibly of great antiquity, particularly if we adopt the principle that whatever is very silly is necessarily very old.

Taken as a whole these hymns, particularly those of the Rig-Veda, are certainly older than any other poetry we possess in India, nay, older than any literary composition we possess of any of the Aryan nations in Asia or Europe. Their real interest, however, consists not only in their age, but in the simplicity and naturalness of their poetical addresses to the most striking phenomena of nature by which the Aryan settlers found themselves surrounded in India and in which and behind which they recognised unseen agents by whom both their physical and their moral life were powerfully influenced.

If all books have their fates, the oldest book of the world, the Veda, has certainly had the most extraordinary fate. It was known to exist and people began to write about it, long before it had been seen or handled by any European. I remember Baron Bunsen telling me how his chief object in arranging to go to India with his pupil, Mr. Astor, was to see whether there really was such a book in existence. By consulting the *Lettres édifiantes* he might have known that it was in existence as a real book, and had been seen and handled by some of the Catholic missionaries in India. But though seen, not a line of it had ever been published, still less translated, because native scholars willing as they might be to help missionaries and others in reading the Laws of Manu, the Mahâbhârata and Râmây*an*a, were most decidedly unwilling to help them to an understanding of the Veda. There were, no doubt, many reasons for it, one of them being possibly that there were few, if any, Brâhmans at the beginning of this century, who were able to translate the Veda themselves. There were many who knew it or large portions of it by heart, and could recite the hymns at sacrifices and public or private gatherings, but they did not even profess that they understood it. They were proud to know it by heart and by sound, and there were some who actually thought that the hymns would lose their magic power, if recited by one who understood their meaning. Manuscripts were never very numerous, and even when one of them fell into the hands of Europeans, they soon found that, without a commentary, the hymns baffled all endeavours at translation.

During all that time the most exaggerated ideas were spread about the Vedas. The Brâhmans themselves declared that they contained the oldest divine revelation, that they were not the compositions of human authors, but the work of Brahman, the Supreme Spirit, who had revealed them to inspired sages or Rishis, seers. European scholars were carried away for a time by the hope that they would find in these Vedas, if not the jabberings of the Pithecanthropoi, at least the earliest flashes of thoughts of an awakening humanity, the faint echoes of a primordial wisdom going back to the very beginning of human life on earth, " when the morning stars sang together and all the sons of God shouted for joy."

When at last not only the texts but the immense Sanskrit commentary also of the most important, the Rig-Veda, had been published, people began to see that there was little of primeval, mysterious wisdom to be found in the Vedic hymns, but only the simplest thoughts that must have passed through the minds of the Rishis when they began to ponder on the great phenomena of nature which every morning and night, every spring and winter were unfolded before their eyes. No superhuman revelation was required for that kind of poetry. Nothing could be clearer than that the constant theme of these Vedic songs were sunrise and morning, day and night, earth and the rivers, storms, lightning, rain, sunset and night. Even this was for a time stoutly denied by writers who did not know the Sanskrit alphabet. But what else was there to interest the ancient Âryas? It is true that even the Brâhmans themselves protested against the Western scholars whose translations seemed to reduce their sacred hymns to the low level of mere descriptions of nature.* We are not and never have been, they said, mere sun-worshippers or fire-worshippers, or rain-worshippers, but sun, fire, and sky were only symbols to

* Kâmesvar Aiyar, Sandhyâvandana, pp. 58, 105, 113.

us of the Godhead, of one and the same Divine Being in his manifold manifestations. In one sense they were certainly right, but I doubt whether many of the much abused Western scholars had ever denied this. Many things have to be taken as understood, and Western scholars evidently took it for granted that when the Vedic poets addressed their hymns to the dawn, to the sun, the sky, the storm-winds, the earth, or the rain, they did not simply mean the fiery ball that rose in the morning and vanished at night, or the blue sky, or the soil on which they stood, or the rain that had fertilised the soil. The very fact that they addressed these phenomena of nature with the pronoun of the second person, changed them at once into persons, or what were called Devatâs, deities, and thus the saying of one of their old grammarians, Yâska, is justified that whatever object is addressed in these Vedic hymns, is to be called its Devatâ—or deity. Later on it came to be recognised that there was even a deeper ground for this deification, and that the necessities of language, that is, of thought, did not allow at first of any names being formed, except names of agent. Dyaus, masc., for instance, the lighter, was earlier than Dyaus, fem., what is lighted up, the sky.

If we take some of the most ancient and most

popular daily prayers, used in the daily Sandhyâ-vandana,* we find that one of them is the famous Gâyatrî, addressed to Savit*ri*, the sun :

"We meditate on the adorable light of the divine Savit*ri*, that he may rouse our thoughts."

This Savit*ri*, the sun, is, of course, more than the fiery ball that rises from the sea or over the hills, but nevertheless the real sun serves as a symbol, and it was that symbol which suggested to the suppliant the divine power manifested in the sun. Hence almost everything that could be predicated of the sun was predicated of Savit*ri* also, whatever was true of the sky, Dyaus, fem., was supposed to be true of Dyaus, masc., Zeus or Jupiter also. As early an authority as Kâtyâyana in his Index to the Rig-Veda declared that all the gods invoked in the Vedic hymns can be reduced to three, to Agni, fire and light on earth, to Vâyu, air, in the atmosphere, and to Sûrya, sun, in the sky, but he adds that all three are in the end meant for one, for Pra*g*âpati, the Lord of creation.

* Sandhyâ is derived from Sandhi, literally the joining, the coming together of day and night, or night and day. Sandhi-velâ is twilight, and Sandhyâ has the same meaning. Sandhyâ-vandana was originally the twilight-worship, the morning and evening prayer, to which a third was added (the Mâdhyâhnika) the noon prayer, when the sun culminated. These prayers were once incumbent on every Brâhman, though they have now assumed a very perfunctory form, or are omitted altogether.

And later on he says, that there is only one deity, namely the Great Self, Mahân Âtmâ, and some say that he is the sun, (Sûrya), or that the sun is he. One of the prayers in the Sândhyâvandana begins with Asâv Âdityo Brahma, that Âditya (sun) is Brahman, and in the Taitt. Upanishad, viii., 8, it is said, "He who dwells in man and he who dwells in the sun, are one and the same." The same idea may be likewise deduced from the hymns themselves. In X., 158, 1, we read, "May the sun (Sûrya) protect us from the sky, the wind (Vâyu) from mid-air, and fire (Agni) from the earth;" whereas in another hymn, 115, 1, we read, "the Sun is the Self or soul of all that moves and rests." Here we can clearly watch the gradual transition from the visible sun to the invisible agent of the sun which may have taken centuries to evolve, and if we consider how almost everything on earth is dependent on the sun for its very life, we can understand how a perfectly natural road led from the sun as seen in heaven, to the sun as the highest, the supreme, nay, in the end, as the only deity. This religious and philosophical development of the concept of the sun did not, however, prevent its simultaneous mythological growth. This is the famous Solar Theory, which, no doubt, has been much exaggerated, but which, if properly understood, admits, we know, of cheap cavil, but never of refutation; nay, which, if but rightly understood, has really received more support from its supposed critics than from its originators and supporters. One of the most intelligible names given to the sun was A*s*va, the racer, or Dadhikrâvan or Vâ*g*in, horse. And while at one time the sun was a racer, at another the sun was conceived as approaching men and standing on a golden chariot which was drawn by horses, as in Greek mythology. Thus we read, Rig-Veda I, 35, 2: "The god Savit*ri* (the sun), approaching on the dark-blue sky, sustaining mortals and immortals, comes on his golden chariot, beholding all the worlds."

I have been assured that the noisy cannonade which was directed for years against this explanation of Vedic and Aryan mythology, was really meant as a kind of salute; but I should have much preferred a few twenty-pounders to test the solidity of my entrenched position. When at last I was charged with never having taken any notice of certain illustrious critics, it seemed to me but courteous to respond to that appeal. But there was really little to answer because there was so little difference between my critics and myself. They evidently thought that I was opposed to their anthropological theories, whereas on the contrary I rejoiced in them, whenever they rested on scholarly evidence. I had myself dabbled in the grammar of the Mohawk and Hottentot languages, because I considered grammar a *sine qua non* of mythology, nor was I much disturbed when my Sanskrit scholarship was found fault with by critics who did not know the Sanskrit alphabet. That real Sanskrit scholars should have differed on certain etymologies, was quite another thing, nor was it difficult to come to an understanding with them. Either they were mistaken on certain points or I was, but no real Sanskrit scholar would ever join in the clamour of those who maintained that Greek, Latin, and Teutonic mythology had quite a different origin from that of the Veda. Such things pass and are soon forgotten, and no one who, like myself, remembers the time when Bopp was laughed at by classical scholars for the foolish idea that Greek and Latin grammar should be explained by a comparison with Sanskrit would be much disturbed by those who did not blush to say that there was only one tenable equation between the names of classical and Vedic deities, viz. Dyaus = Zeus. But have those ready writers ever reflected what such an admission would really mean, and how it would disable the whole of their machinery? What would happen if the name of Jehovah, or even of Yahveh turned up suddenly in the Veda? Thinking is difficult, but it is sometimes useful. Such things will be remembered hereafter among the Curiosities of Literature. No one is infallible, but because we have occasionally a fall on the ice, it does not follow that we must not skate or even cut figures on the ice. There is plenty of work to do for those who are willing to work either at the language of the Rig-Veda, or at that of the Maoris, but without some of that grammatical drudgery, I doubt whether mere assertions, or repeating the opinions of others, will really forward our knowledge of the *origines* of our own race.

It is surely as clear as daylight to anybody who will read a number of the hymns of the Rig-Veda that they refer to the principal phenomena of nature, and that in that respect they require no antecedents, but are intelligible to any child. Yet for a number of years there has been a constant outcry from certain anthropologists, who asserted that the Vedic hymns were modern in spirit, modern in language, and modern in their pantheon, and that this pantheon had nothing whatever to do with the phenomena of nature, and had no relationship whatever with the gods of the other Aryan nations, particularly of Greeks, Romans, and Teutons. They looked upon the Vedic religion as the last phase in a development, the earlier stages of which had to be studied among savage races, such as the *well-known* Kamilaroi, Wiraturei, Waihvun,

&c. Have they forgotten this? It is true, no doubt, that the ideas expressed in the Veda presupposed a long development, even a period of savagery, considering that all civilised nations must once have been less civilised, uncivilised, or even savages. There are quite sufficient survivals of savagery even in the Veda itself, only it is Aryan savagery, not savagery of the Pacific Islanders, African negroes, or Dravidians. If only some cases could be produced in which the Australian blacks shared any of the ideas of the Veda, or displayed similar ideas, only more savage, every true scholar would welcome them with open arms. Our expectations have been raised to a very high pitch in that direction, and I still hope that in time they may be fulfilled. In the meantime it is fortunate that the mere clamour against the Veda has at last subsided, so that now people only marvel how it could ever have arisen.

Most of the names of the Vedic deities implied at first activity only, but very soon personality also, and what is most important, some of them were found to be exactly the same in Sanskrit, in Greek, Latin, German, and Slavonic, being only changed in every one of these languages according to the phonetic rules peculiar to each. Such verbal coincidences had to be accounted for, and they could not be accounted for except by the admission that there was once a period, a truly historical period, during which the framers of these mythological names and the believers in these physical powers, or, as we are accustomed to call them, these natural Gods or Devas, were still living together as one language, people, or nation. Such an admission, inevitable as it was in the eyes of all true scholars, roused at the time a certain dislike and incredulity among those who like to shrug their shoulders at every new discovery. Forgetful of the fact that proper names in all languages undergo certain phonetic changes which do not apply to ordinary appellatives, they thought they could belittle the value of such equations as Sarameyâ = *Ἑρμείας*, Saranyû = *Ἐρινύς*, Haritas = *Χάριτες* by pointing out that strictly speaking the Greek forms should have been *Ἑρεμείας* and *Ἑρινύς*, while the Greek Charites, though identical in names, seemed to resist all efforts to trace them back to the same source from which sprang the bright horses of the sun-god.

This cheap scepticism, however, or, as it is now called, this higher criticism, may safely be said to belong to the past. I am old enough to remember the conversion of such giants as Gottfried Hermann, Otfried Müller, and Welcker to the principles of scholarship, as taught by Bopp, Grimm, and others. That was indeed a real triumph. In 1825,

Otfried Müller, the real founder of a scientific mythology (*wissenschaftliche Mythologie*) was sighing for a translation of the Rig-Veda. In 1899, when a great part of it has been made accessible by the patient labours of English, French, and German scholars, some writers who call themselves mythologists, seem to take a pride in ignoring the existence of the Veda. How far we have advanced since 1825, may be gathered from a statement to which I should be very sorry to affix a name, "that the only generally accepted case of similarity between Vedic and classical mythological names was that of Dyaush-pitar, *Ζεῦς πατήρ*, and Jupiter." Has Benfey taught in vain? Even in 1839, Benfey (*Wörterbuch*, ii., 334) knew that Ushas was = Eos, Agni (fire) = ignis, (ibid., ii., 217), Sûrya = Helios (ibid., i., 458), to say nothing of later equations which, even if disapproved of, or disproved, would leave the general principles of Comparative Mythology exactly as they were fifty years ago. Has all this been forgotten, or never been learnt?

The discovery of Vedic literature which had retained the clearest traces of a common Aryan mythology, even if no equation besides that of Dyaush-pitar = *Ζεῦς πατήρ* had survived, was really the discovery of a new world, of a *terra antiquis incognita*, and gave us a glimpse at a whole period of thought, of which no relics whatever could be found anywhere else, whether in Greece, Italy, or Germany.

But highly interesting as these Vedic hymns are to us, in spite of, or, I should say, on account of their simplicity and childishness, anybody who came to know them at first hand had to confess that they seem quite unfit to satisfy the religious cravings of a later generation. They contain praises of the physical gods, they implore their help, they render thanks for benefits supposed to have come from their hands, light and life from Dyaus, rain and food from a closely related power, called Indra, warmth and light from Agni, new life every morning from Ushas or Eos. All this is historically and psychologically full of interest, but there is but little, except here and there, of exalted religious thought, of poetry or philosophy, still less of any records of historical events. Besides, their language is so difficult that, as yet, it makes a satisfactory translation of the whole Veda a perfect impossibility. This may seem surprising in the days when hieroglyphic and cuneiform inscriptions have been so readily translated. But the fact is that most of those inscriptions are very straightforward, they hardly contain a conditional or a relative sentence. We read of Kings and Kings of Kings, of their battles from year to year, of the towns they founded, of the conquests they made, the captives they led away, the tribute they received and so on, and yet even such simple statements vary very considerably from year to year according as they are translated by bold or timid scholars. The Vedic hymns on the contrary, even when we understand every word of them, remain very obscure in their structure or construction; and though their texts are very firmly established from the time they had first been reduced to writing and made the subject of the most minute grammatical study in India, even before the spreading of Buddhism, it is clear that before that time, when the Vedic texts existed in oral tradition only, they must have been exposed to many vicissitudes. There are verbal emendations so palpable that we can hardly understand how the mistakes could have arisen, and could have been tolerated for one moment. Besides that, there are evidently old and new hymns, yet all of them are recognised as belonging to the Veda, ever since the Vedic hymns were systematically collected.

The attempts that have been made to translate the Vedic hymns may be divided into four periods. The first consisted of those who followed Sâya*n*a's great Sanskrit commentary. This was the method followed by Rosen in 1830 and 1838, and again, in 1850, by H. H. Wilson. It was soon found out, however, that highly useful, nay indispensable, as the traditional interpretation of Sâyana might be, it was in many places quite impossible to follow him, because the true meaning was too clear, and that adopted by Sâyana, too absurd. Rosen already used very freely the privilege of the scholar to choose between what is rational and what is not. Wilson had a stronger faith in Sâyana, and gave us in his translation the traditional rendering, even where his own sound sense rebelled against it.

There were others again who went into the other extreme, and from sheer despair at Sâyana's commentary, translated the Veda according to what they thought it ought to mean. Langlois, a professor of eloquence at Paris, carried this principle very far indeed, yet we find that his translation is still followed by some writers on ancient religion and mythology.

In the meantime a new school was slowly gaining ground who held that the only satisfactory way of translating the Veda was to construct, first of all, a complete *Index Verborum**, to examine

* I still have a letter from the late M. Bergaigne, in which he asks when my Index would be published, and adds : " Je m'étais décidé pendant ces vacances à écrire tout le Rig-Véda sur des fiches, et à me composer ainsi un index qui pût me permettre des essais d'interprétation indépendante. Je suis arrivé à la moitié de ce travail, et grâce à la rapidité que je suis parvenu à atteindre, et aussi à une grande puissance de travail, je puis le ter-

every passage in which the same word occurs, and then to assign that meaning to each word which would satisfy the context wherever it occurred. I published such an *Index Verborum* at the end of my edition of Sâya*n*a's commentary, and it is easy to see the influence which it exercised at once on the translations of the Rig-Veda which we owe to Grassmann, to Ludwig, and to Ralph T. H. Griffith, and to others who tried their hands on single hymns or single verses. Still greater was the influence exercised by the Sanskrit Dictionary of Boehtlingk and Roth, and the Vedic Vocabulary of Grassmann, though, of course, neither the one nor the other professed to give a complete index of every word and every form in every passage in which it occurred.

The method which I recommended, and which I followed in the specimens published (in 1859, in my "History of Ancient Sanskrit Literature," in 1869, in the "Hymns to the Storm-gods," and again in the "Sacred Books of the East," 1891), was so tedious, however, that few scholars only felt tempted to follow it. Professor Roth, the

miner en moins d'un mois . . . S'il n'était pas trop exiger, je vous prierais de me dire aussi si vous citez tous les emplois de chaque mot *sans aucune exception*, ou si vous êtes départi de cette rigueur pour les mots très usuels, et enfin si vous adoptez l'ordre alphabétique pur et simple." I could answer all these questions in the affirmative.

scholar most qualified, through his lexical labours, to give us a real translation of the Veda, was honest enough to say again and again that such a work belonged to the next generation of Sanskrit scholars, and to the next century. I myself, having accepted the appointment to a new professorship of Comparative Philology at Oxford, had other things to do, and after I had given the best part of my life to supplying the materials necessary for such a task, I hoped that the ambition of younger scholars would have been roused to undertake this no doubt difficult, but very grateful work. I did not go so far as to say, as has been supposed, that every word, whenever it occurred, should again and again be followed by every translator through all its hiding places. A number of words have once for all been fixed in their meanings, and when that was the case, they were naturally passed, as known to every Sanskrit scholar. Still the mere physical exertion in collecting all parallel passages became too much for me, and I had reluctantly to give it up to younger and more vigorous hands.

We are now at the beginning of a new era in Vedic scholarship whenever the Complete Concordance, promised by Professor Lanman, shall have been published. This will be a gigantic work, but it is really the *sine qua non* for the Vedic exegesis of the future, and we may expect much help from it. But though many passages may be unravelled by a more complete intercomparison, my own impression is that, through the influence of a long continued oral tradition a great amount of real corruption has crept into our texts which no amount of conjectural emendation will ever entirely remove. This may sound very discouraging, but fortunately, after deducting ever so much that is hopeless, there remains enough of the 1,017 hymns to give us that insight into the first development of religious thought in India and indirectly among the Aryan nations in general, which is so full of interest to us psychologically, even more than historically. So many conflicting theories have lately been started about the origin of religion, that it must seem to many people as if, like other beginnings, that of religion also was really beyond our grasp. But this is to a great extent our own fault, because philosophers are bent on discovering the origin of religion, instead of being satisfied with studying the origin of religions, or of each individual religion with which it is possible to do so, that is of which we possess old literary documents. For that purpose the study of the Veda is invaluable. But who would try to discover the origin of Islam, without studying the Korân? or of Buddhism without knowing the Suttas? Who would offer an opinion about the beginning of Christianity, unless he had read the Gospels? even then, it is well known how far removed the Gospels are from the Nativity, and the Korân from the Hejrah. But if we approach the religions of Greeks and Romans, where shall we find the Sibylline leaves telling us of their real parentage? If there lived many heroes before Agamemnon, there lived many poets and prophets before Homer; but who can pierce through the cruel darkness that hides them from our sight?

And what shall we do when we have to deal with religious customs and mythological lore of savage, uncivilised, and illiterate tribes? A study of their languages is no doubt an immense help towards a correct understanding of their traditions; and we cannot be sufficiently grateful to men like Hahn, Codrington, Tregear, and others who did not shrink from that drudgery, before writing on the myths or customs of uncivilised tribes. The most useful materials may be found where some popular poetry has been preserved to the present day, as among the Maoris or of some of the Ugro-Finnic tribes.

It is well known how much labour has been spent on establishing the date and the authenticity of the Vedic hymns. Their authenticity is now admitted by all Sanskrit scholars. Their date has been fixed by me in my "History of Ancient Sanskrit Literature" (1859) at about 1200 to 1500 B.C. But though this date has met with very general acceptance, I am the very last person to consider it as firmly established, and I have again and again given my reasons why I should gladly escape from the force of my own arguments. If other scholars have clamoured for a higher age, for 2,000 or 5,000 B.C., they are quite welcome to these dates if they can establish them by any kind of historical evidence, and not merely by their wishes; but as yet these guesses are outside the sphere of practical scholarship, quite as much as the date assigned by a Babylonian scholar to the immigration of the Âryas into India, so late as 500 or at the utmost 600 B.C.!

But no literary or traditional documents which we possess, whether in Greek or Latin or in any other Oriental language, to say nothing of barbarous dialects, bring us so near, if not to the origin, at least to the early historical development of any of the ancient religions of mankind as the hymns of the Veda. If the study of single religions must precede the study of religion in general, nowhere can we get so near to the origin of any single religion as in the hymns of the Rig-Veda. Other religions may be older, and religion by itself may be beyond all conception old, but no single religion, as far as I know, has been preserved in documents so old, and so near to the very cradle of a religion as that which we see growing before our eyes in the Veda. Let those who want to know the origin of religion, *a priori*, take refuge in metaphysics; but those who care to understand the origin of one single religion will find no better oracle to consult than the poems of the Vedic Rishis.

The chronological date of the Vedic hymns, which has been fixed by some at 1200, by others at 2000, nay at 4500 B.C., are, no doubt, very uncertain, and can be no more than constructive. But though Egyptian and Babylonian dates go far beyond any date in India, we can see more of the real beginnings of religion in India than even in Egypt or Babylon. Nor would anybody accept the principle laid down by students of the religion of savages, that whatever is savage or barbarous in religion, must be old. This is a major premiss that would play fearful havoc with our chronology.

What is quite clear is that, between the Vedic hymns and the next period, that of the prose Brâhma*n*as, there is a great gulf. The hymns of the three Vedas had not only been collected, such as we have them, but had already been invested with a divine authority, such as is seldom ascribed to works of recent date. Besides, it is clear that the language of the hymns had often been completcly misunderstood by the authors of the Brâhma*n*as, and that a new style had sprung up in the place of that of the old poetical compositions. From the time of the Brâhma*n*as, which precede the rise of Buddhism (500 B.C.) to the present day, the old hymns of the Veda have retained their unique position in India. Invested with the character of a divine revelation they have been to the people in India what the Bible has been to us.

And yet how different is this Bible of India from all other Bibles! No doubt we meet in the Veda with some exalted, and some very abstract ideas also, but its general character is very different. It is simple, straightforward, natural, without any attempt at systematic treatment, without any effort for poetical beauty. When we take day and night, spring and winter, as they come and go, we shall find in the hymns thoughts such as would naturally spring up in the minds of any unsophisticated observers who felt that there must be something behind the visible world, some powers or persons directing the course of nature, possibly some power even beyond the powers, whom they called Devas or Bright ones. It was chiefly the phenomena which recurred regularly that impressed themselves on their minds and evoked in time the idea of order and law as pervading the whole of nature, even its very thunderstorms and lightnings.

There is hardly a language in which sun and

moon, day and night, dawn and fire have not received their names, many of which, on account of their multiplicity, led almost inevitably to mythological metamorphosis. Anthropology has clearly shown that the idea that exceptional events such as meteors, earthquakes, hurricanes, lightning, eclipses of sun or moon, furnished the first impulses to religion and mythology is no longer tenable, even though it has, or rather seemed to have, the often quoted support of Seneca. If we may judge by what has been observed among uncivilised as well as civilised races—for even civilised races must once have been uncivilised—regularity attracts attention first and irregularity follows, or, as it has been more tersely expressed, the Gods come first, the Devils second, though it is quite true that in later times Devil-worship may have become more important, or, at least, more prominent than the worship of the Gods. Of these so-called prehistoric periods of human thought, however, we must always speak with great reserve. We must never forget that they are constructions of our own, and that we shall never be able to appeal to historical facts in support of our theories. Facts are given us for the first time during the Etymological Period of languages, and afterwards, but at a much later time, by the scant remains to be gathered from the Sacred Books of the East.

And here the Vedic hymns will always hold their foremost place. However late we may place this systematic collection, their composition carries us back far beyond the chronological limits reached by any other documents. And what gives an additional interest to these Vedic fragments is that they allow us an insight into the earliest development not only of religion, but of mythology also. We see superstitions springing up by the side of religion, demons by the side of gods, agriculture by the side of the chase, bows and arrows by the side of the stone-weapons (A*s*ani), such as Indra hurled against V*ri*tra in his fight against the powers of darkness. Though the conception of the rainbow being the bow of the god of the sky is not to be found in the Rig-Veda, bows and arrows were well known to the worshippers of the Vedic gods. The Science of Mythology, after tossing about for centuries on the ocean of mere conjectures, has at last found its compass. We no longer see in it, like Bacon, mere lessons of morality in the disguise of fables, or broken rays of a primeval revelation, or misunderstood fragments of the Old Testament, still less recollections of a period of savagery to be studied in the myths and customs of modern savages, or survivals of a belief in amulets and magic incantations, generally the very latest outcome of mythology in its historical development, though I believe there are still survivals of defenders of every one of these time-hallowed theories. We know now, and we know it chiefly from the lessons taught us by the Veda, that our Aryan mythology, and to a certain extent our ancient Aryan religion also, took its origin from a poetical interpretation of the great phenomena of nature, personified and named as the chief agents of the eternal physical drama, enacted before us every day, every month, every season, every year, and we know also that this broad stream of mythology, when once started, was open to ever so many tributaries, superstitions, customs, vain genealogies, sorceries, idolatries of every kind, whether springing from fancies and imaginations, or from downright falsehoods and impositions. All these things are apt to be absorbed by mythology, and must be taken into account when we attempt a scientific analysis of it. It must not be supposed, however, that the attempt to find the key of Aryan mythology in fetishism, totemism, shamanism, and wherever it was *not* to be found, have been entirely wasted. A reconnoitring party, even though it return disappointed, has rendered real service by showing where the enemy is not to be found, and that service has certainly been rendered by the exploring parties who thought they could discover in Africa, America, or Australia what was ready to hand in India, Greece, Italy, and among Celtic, Teutonic, and Slavonic races.

People continue to write as if there was still some mystery about the Rig-Veda. There may have been when we began, in the days of Rosen and Burnouf, but there is no longer. The tools are there, all that is now required is honest work, and there is plenty of it, even if there were more real labourers and not merely gleaners than we have at present. It would be by no means difficult to put together a number of hymns which would at once settle the question by showing us the Hindu mind such as it really was during the Vedic period, and impressed by the grand sights of nature that passed before it day and night.

The same story is told again and again, and wherever we open the Rig-Veda, the same daily drama in its successive stages seems enacted before our eyes. Some people, more particularly the late M. Bergaigne, have been disconcerted by the many allusions not only to the sights of nature, but to the daily sacrifices also which occur in these hymns, but they evidently did not realise that, however complicated and technical the sacrifice had become before the time when these Vedic hymns were collected, there is nothing incongruous between praise and sacrifice. Sacrifice was a very natural occupation for the Vedic savages, as it is among savages at the present day. Whether a man who can describe the daily sunrise in artificial metres belongs to a more primitive humanity than a man who marks the stations of the sun, the phases of the moon, or the return of the seasons to say his prayers and pour out his libations, Sanskrit scholars would gladly leave to members of Ethnological Societies to determine. Whether the Veda is primeval or not, is another question that may likewise be left to those who know what primeval really means.

The grave mistake to be guarded against is to suppose that the Veda is an exclusively liturgical book, monotonous throughout, and belongs therefore to a late liturgical age. Savages, as ethnologists themselves have told us, are often very punctilious ritualists, and if we only consider how essential the Vedic sacrificial system was to the Âryas of India in determining times and seasons, in fact, in laying the first foundations of a well-regulated society, we shall no longer be surprised at the numerous liturgical allusions which occur in the Vedic hymns, nor on the other hand see more of liturgy in them than there really is. Whoever has read if only the first hymn of the Rig-Veda*, will know how many words in it have

* Giuseppe Turrini, *Raccolta degli Inni del Vêda*, Libro I, Fascicolo I, Bologna, 1899.

a liturgical meaning, but nowhere have those liturgical ideas obscured the original character of the Vedic gods, as being the agents or actors in the physical drama of nature which first made the simple sons of nature ponder on the meaning of day and night, of sun and moon, of earth and sky, in fact of all that made them wonder, and turn their thoughts beyond the horizon of the visible world.

I think it may be best if I give here a few of those Vedic hymns. They have a right to a place among my Indian Friends. They have been with me for many years. They have often roused me in the morning, they have soothed me in the evening. I have tried to make them out as one tries to make out the character of a friend, even when at times one feels puzzled with him. I have always trusted them with good intentions, and if some of their utterances for a long time remained dark and still remain dark, are there not some dark corners in most of our friends, nay, even in ourselves?

It has been truly said that books are our best friends. We see more of them than of any other friends, and even if we get tired of them at times, they are always ready to renew their friendship. People of the world may wonder what we can see to attract us in such books as the Rig-Veda and to keep us faithful to them to the end. But if they tried, they would find that there are few of the great books of the world which are not worth knowing, and that there are many which deserve our friendship, our love, and our lasting gratitude.

I shall select these Vedic friends at random, following, however, the guidance of an old grammarian, Yâska, who tells us in what succession the Vedic gods appear on the heavenly stage every day, and particularly in the morning. It is in the morning, when light and life return that the bright beings, the Devas, are seen, and the daily revelation of another world takes place, while the various aspects of the new light are personified in the principal gods of the Veda. The order in which they appear, according to Yâska is : A*s*vinau, day and night, Ushas, dawn, Sûryâ, wife of the sun, V*ri*shskapâyî, wife of V*ri*shakapi, doubtful, Sara*n*yû, early dawn, Erinys, Savit*ri*, the enlivening sun, Bhaga, the sun before sunrise, Sûrya, the risen sun.

We begin with the two A*s*vins whom Yâska places at the head of the daily procession of the Devas, the Bright Ones.

HYMN TO THE ASVINS, DAY AND NIGHT.

No Vedic gods have been so completely misunderstood as these heavenly twins, and misunderstood by the Brâhmans themselves. Still even these misunderstandings are instructive. The Asvins were taken for a pair of horsemen, though it is well known that riders on horseback occur very seldom in the Veda, so that some scholars have wrongly maintained that riding on horseback was altogether unknown in Vedic times. The Asvins were taken by native exegetes for old heroes or kings, and why they should have formed part of the Vedic gods who appear in the morning and the evening*, was never so much as asked. Besides, Asvin would be a very strange name for rider, and would much rather convey the meaning of a descendant or connection of Asva, or Asvâ, i. e. the Horse, or the Mare, one of the many mythological names, as we saw, of the sun and the dawn. Being a couple the Asvins were really the oldest representatives of the couple of day and night, travelling always on their ordained path from morning till evening, the same path on which Agni also travels † in his character of the light of day. Thus they were very naturally mixed up with many of the daily adventures of the Sun and

* Rig-Veda X, 39, 1. † Rig-Veda III, 29, 6.

the Dawn *. Dyaus is called the father of the A*s*vins (Rig-Veda X, 61, 4), the Dawn their mother, while under another name, as Sûryâ, she is represented as the daughter of Savit*ri* and as the beloved of the A*s*vins †. Another poet says that the Dawn is born, when the A*s*vins have harnessed their chariot, and that Day and Night, again the A*s*vins, spring from Vivasvat ‡, the shining sun. As Sara*n*yû, Erinys, also is called the mother of the A*s*vins, she must likewise have been another form of the Dawn, in her varying aspects.

The stories about the A*s*vins when they have once become mythological characters, heroes, saviours, and physicians, are endless, but they need not detain us. The important point is to perceive their physical background, and that can always be discovered even behind the thick veil of legend. Nothing is more instructive for the student of mythology than to see how this natural conception of Day and Night, of Light and Darkness, as the A*s*vins, becomes the germ from which spring in time ever so many half-legendary and even half-historical fables, the so-called Itihâras.

Most of the hymns addressed to the A*s*vins are very tedious, and repeat again and again the nu-

* Rig-Veda III, 20, 1. † Rig-Veda I, 116, 17.
‡ Rig-Veda X, 39, 12.

merous miracles which they performed and the kindnesses which they showed to their friends and worshippers. I give here one short hymn only (V, 76), enough, however, to show what physical background there was for them, a background which in many cases had entirely vanished from the purview of the Vedic Rishis, but which is clear enough to the student of mythology.

I have endeavoured in these translations to keep strictly to the metre of the original, which is not always easy. I must therefore crave the indulgence of my readers for certain infelicities of expression which I could not avoid without departing too much from the original.

HYMN TO THE ASVINS, DAY AND NIGHT.

1.

Agni shines forth, the shining face of Ushas *,
The priests' god-loving voices have ascended,
O Asvins, on your chariot hither tending,
Come to our overflowing morn-libation.

2.

The quick do not despise our ready offering;
They have been praised, and are now near beside us;
Early and late they hasten to our succour,
The worshipper's best friends against all evil.

* Dawn.

3.

Come hither then at milking-time, at breakfast,
Come here at noon, and come at sunset also,
By day, by night, come with your happy succour;
Our draught has always brought the Asvins hither.

4.

This place, forsooth, has always been your dwelling,
The houses here, O Asvins, and this shelter;
Come from high heaven then, and from the mountain *,
Come from the waters, bringing food and vigour.

5.

May we attain the Asvins' newest blessings,
Their happy guidance, health and wealth bestowing;
Immortals, bring us riches, bring us heroes,
And all that here on earth can make us happy.

If we remember that these twins were originally meant for morning and evening, the process by which they gradually became what they are in this hymn and in other hymns more full of personal legends, is most instructive to watch. That the Asvins were originally meant for morning and evening, or for the two halves of the diurnal twenty-four hours, cannot be called in question, unless another germ-idea is first suggested for them. But then, is it not instructive to see how day and night simply by being addressed in the

* The cloud.

second person became personified, became human and even divine, and were called by a name which would be unintelligible unless we remembered that the sun had once been called Asva, the runner, and that Asvâ, the mare, had been used as a not uncommon name of the Dawn. These beings who seemed to move on the same daily path as the sun, or to have been born of the Dawn, called Asvâ, were then called the sons or friends of the Dawn, Asvinau, or the horsemen, as representing the two phases of the sun, or of the horse; or, as Yâska says, Nir. XII, 2, the sun of night and the sun of morning. Their three-wheeled chariot is golden, and in a single day goes round heaven and earth. And when that first metamorphosis had once been effected, when Day and Night had once become a pair of runners, ever returning to the same spot in the morning, almost every blessing that comes from day and night, particularly health and length of days, would naturally be ascribed to them. Thus they gradually assumed the general character of saviours and of physicians, and ever so many beings who were rescued from dangers or from death, whether the setting sun, or the setting moon, or the setting year, were supposed to have been rescued by them. Their chief work is to restore life, and to renew youth, or to give sight to the blind. In many cases the names of the heroes rescued or helped by them speak for themselves, and leave no doubt, in the minds of Sanskrit scholars at least, that they represent physical phenomena, a fact admitted in this case even by so great a sceptic as Bergaigne. Only it must not be supposed that, because we can explain some of their names, we ought to be able to explain them all. The Brâhmans themselves had long forgotten the original purport of these names, and when that was the case, they did not hesitate to give us as facts what were merely their conjectures. As one of the characteristic features of the A*s*vins was that they always returned, Nâsatya, the returning (*νόστιοι* from *νόστος*, homeward journey) would seem a very applicable name. But ancient grammarians quoted by Yâska, VI, 13, explained it by Na + Asatya, not untrue, or by Nasikâprabhava, born of the nose. Yet Yâska himself had a very just perception of the nature of the A*s*vins. He quotes various opinions of his predecessors who saw in them heaven and earth, or day and night, or sun and moon, or, lastly, two pious kings. Only this is not a question so much of *aut-aut*, as of *et-et*. They were all this, only from different points of view, and this comprehensiveness is one of the most important features of ancient mythological thought. However startling this may sound to those who form their theories without any reference to historical facts, it is really one of the most important keys for unlocking the riddles of the most ancient periods of mythology, and should be carefully distinguished from what is meant by the syncretism of much later times.

HYMN TO USHAS, DAWN.

Next follows Ushas, the Dawn, identical in name, *pace* M. Reinach, with the Greek Eos. She is represented as the most beautiful heavenly apparition among the gods in their procession from East to West. She is called the daughter of Dyaus, the sister of Agni, also his beloved, according to the changing aspects in which the sun of the morning and the dawn presented themselves to the fancy of the Vedic poets. I subjoin the translation of a hymn addressed to Ushas from the first Ma*nd*ala, hymn 123.

1.

Dakshi*n*â's * roomy chariot has been harnessed,
And the immortal gods have mounted on it,
The growing Dawn, free from the dark oppressor,
Stepped forth to spy for the abode of mortals.

* Name of the Dawn. It requires a considerable acquaintance with phonetic laws to doubt the identity of the names Ushas in Sanskrit and Eos in Greek. Yet I believe that even this has been achieved by those who seem to imagine that scepticism is the best proof of knowledge.

2.

The mighty woke before all other creatures,
She wins the race, and always conquers riches;
The Dawn looks out, young and reviving ever,
She came the first here to our morning prayers.

3.

When thou, O Dawn, to-day dividest treasures,
Thou goddess, nobly born, among all mortals,
May Savit*ri* *, the god, the friend of homesteads,
Proclaim us innocent before the sun-god!

4.

To every house is Ahanâ † approaching,
Giving to every day its name and being,
Dyotanâ † came, for ever bent on conquest,
She gets the best of all the splendid treasures.

5.

Varu*n*a's sister, sister thou of Bhaga,
O Sûn*ri*tâ †, O Dawn, sing first at daybreak;
May he fall back, the man that plotteth mischief,
With Dakshi*n*â and car let us subdue him.

6.

Let hymns rise up, let pray'rs rise up together,
The fires have risen, clad in flaring splendour,
The brilliant Dawn displays the lovely treasures
Which had been hidden by the night and darkness.

* Savit*ri*, the sun-god, but distinct from Sûrya, the sun and sun god.

† Name of Dawn.

7.

The one departeth and the other cometh *,
Unlike in hue the two march close together;
One secretly brought night to earth and heaven,
Dawn sparkled forth on her refulgent chariot.

8.

Alike to-day, alike to-morrow also,
They ever follow Varu*n*a's † commandment;
They one by one achieve their thirty Yogans ‡,
And without fail achieve their lord's (Varu*n*a's) commandment §.

9.

She knows the first day's name, and brightly shining,
White she is born to-day, from out the darkness;
The maiden never breaks th' eternal order ||,
And day by day comes to the place appointed.

10.

Proud of thy beauty, maiden-like thou comest,
O goddess to the god ¶ who thee desireth;
A smiling girl, thou openest before him
Thy bosom's splendour, as thou shinest brightly.

* Day and Night, Dawn and Twilight are conceived as sisters, and spoken of as Ahanî, the two days, one bright, the other dark, like the A*s*vins.

† Varu*n*a, sometimes the highest god, whose laws have to be obeyed by all creatures.

‡ Their appointed course.

§ Kratu, thought, will, here command.

|| The order in which the heavenly bodies come and go, which gave the first intimation of order in the universe.

¶ The sun.

11.

Fair as a bride, adorned by loving mother,
Thou showest forth thy form, that they may see it;
Auspicious Dawn, shine forth more wide and brightly,
No other dawns * have ever reached thy splendour.

12.

With horses, cows, and all delightful treasures,
And striving with the rays of yonder Sûrya,
The Dawns depart and come again with splendour,
Bearing auspicious names and forms auspicious.

13.

Obedient to the reins of law eternal,
Grant us auspicious thoughts for our endeavours,
Shine thou upon us, Dawn, thou swift to listen,
May we and all our liberal chieftains prosper!

In spite of all the angry and ill-natured words of M. Bergaigne, I ask once more whether this address to the Dawn is not perfectly natural and intelligible. Whether it required a priest to compose it, or whether any father of a family could have done so, who can tell? And who can tell whether the first priest was not simply the father of a family, who had his fire always burning on the domestic hearth, and who felt grateful for the re-

* Dawn is often spoken of in the plural, being conceived as new every day, or being considered manifold in her wide expanse.

turn of the dawn, which coincided with the kindling of the fire on his hearth. If the morning service was called Pûrvahûti, what is that more than the early calling, Hûti being derived from the same root, Hvê, from which we had before Hot*ri*, the invoker, the priest.

But whatever we may think on that point, it seems perfectly clear that the different names by which the Dawn is here addressed, Ushas, Ahanâ, Dyotanâ, Dakshi*n*â, and Sûn*ri*tâ, were understood as names of the Dawn. But will it be believed, that when the Dawn is addressed in the very first verse by the name of Dakshi*n*â, when her chariot is mentioned, and her stepping forth out of darkness to come to the morning-prayer of the people, M. Bergaigne, always on the look out for priestcraft and ritual, sees in Dakshi*n*â, not the Dawn, but *le salaire du sacrifice ?* He thinks it not impossible that *le salaire du sacrifice* might have been the name of the Dawn, *considérée comme le don céleste accordé pour récompense à l'homme pieux.* But he declines even this small concession, and, if I understand him rightly, he actually takes Dakshi*n*â in the first and fifth verses of our hymn as the salary of the priests. Now it is quite true that Dakshi*n*â has this meaning of salary or gift due to the priest who performs that sacrifice, but that meaning is clearly impossible here. Our hymn contains several unusual names of the Dawn, such as Ahanâ, Dyotanâ, Sûnritâ, all ἅπαξ λεγόμενα, as names of the Dawn, then why not Dakshinâ? Dakshinâ means right, *dexter*, evidently from Daksha, strength, the right hand being the strong or clever hand. It then means southern. It also means the cow, the strong cow which has calves and gives milk (Dakshinâ gâvah, Lâty. VIII, 5), and as such a cow was the most primitive payment (*fee* and *pecu*), it may well have become the regular name for the fee due to the priest. She is celebrated as such in one of the Vedic hymns, X, 107. But however prominent a place may have been assigned to this Dakshinâ, the salary of priests, how could the Dawn have been called the salary? We can hardly explain, why even that salary was called Dakshinâ, unless we suppose that it was meant for the right hand, or *la bonne main*, and in that case Dakshinâ, Dawn, might have been meant for the liberal goddess. But whatever the evolution of the meaning of Dakshinâ may have been *, when she was invoked as Dakshinâ, she could not have been invoked as Salary. I am glad to see that even M. Bergaigne has not been bold enough

* Perhaps it should be remembered that in the Mahâbhârata the wife of Kasyapa, the mother of the Âdityas, was called Dakshâyanî; see Pramatha Nâth Mullick, "Origin of Caste," p. 33.

to translate "*Le large char du Salaire a été attelé,*" but "*Le large char de la Dakshinâ.*" If Dakshinâ were really in that sense an *ἅπαξ λεγόμενον*, surely it is not the only *ἅπαξ λεγόμενον* in the scanty survivals of Vedic poetry. When we read that Dakshinâ was the daughter of Dyaus and the mother of Agni (Rig-Veda III, 58, 1), we need no more to feel convinced that she was meant for the Dawn. Besides, who is the Putro Dakshinâyah, the son of Dakshinâ, if not Agni, the same who brings Dyotani, Rig-Veda III, 58, 1? Another name of the Dawn is Dyotanâ, and who can doubt that it meant the brilliant, i. e. the Dawn. More difficult are the other names Ahanâ, and Sûnritâ.

Ahanâ is clearly connected with Ahan, day, just as our dawn is connected with day. It has long been known that day is not connected with *dies*, as was formerly supposed, but that the root of Goth. dags, day, can only have been dah, or dhah, with double aspirate, to burn, to shine. The loss of an initial d is no doubt quite irregular *, though it can be matched by Goth. tagr, Gr. *δάκρυ*, tear, which in Sanskrit appears as Asru, instead of Dasru. I pointed out long ago, and I have never seen any valid reason to retract it, that in the Greek *δάφνη*, laurel tree, the name of a matutinal goddess, we have the root with its initial d, and that another

* Cf. "Chips," iv., p. 385.

derivation of the same root without the initial d, may be recognised in Athanâ or Athênê.

No one, I thought, could have supposed that I meant to see in this Ahanâ one of the grandest Greek goddesses, Athênê. Why will people so often misunderstand, and then place their misunderstanding on the shoulders of those whom they misunderstand? When I said that Zeus is Dyaus, that Eos is Ushas, that Agni is Ignis, surely I could not have meant that these gods and goddesses migrated bodily from India to Greece and from Greece to India. Why must what seems perfectly clear be said again and again, that the Greek and Indian gods were not beings that ever existed in heaven or on earth, but were mere names, mere creations of the human mind. In all comparative mythological studies we have to look for the germs only, and I see in Ahanâ and Athênê a common germ, that withered on Indian soil, while it assumed the grandest development in Greece.

Surely not even Deva is the same as Deus; though it may be the same sound, it does not represent the same meaning, so that strictly speaking we cannot translate the one by the other. The Greek concept of Zeus also was very different from that of the Vedic Dyaus, as that of Eos from that of Ushas. I never went so far as to claim for

Greek and Vedic deities what might be called personal or bodily identity. I was simply looking for germs which after thousands of years might have developed into a Sûrya in the Veda, and into a Helios in Homer. These very modest claims may possibly surprise my adversaries, for, to judge from their remarks, they evidently imagined that I recognised in Zeus a heavenly king who had migrated from India to Greece, and in the Haritas, the horses of the morning who in their journey to Greece had been metamorphosed into the brilliant children of Helios and Aigle. I even begin to see why what some critics supposed to have been my idea, should have ruffled their temper so much, and I say once more, and I hope for the last time, that I never believed that Athênê lived in the thoughts of Vedic Rishis, nor Varu*n*a in the prayers of Greek priests. No, I am and always have been satisfied with far less. All I stand up for is that, given the sky, the Greeks raised Dyu, sky, to become their Zeus, while the Vedic Rishis made the sky their Dyaus. This Dyaus is superseded in the Veda by his own son, Indra, whereas Zeus in Greece remained to the end the *θεῶν ὕπατος καὶ ἄριστος*. What is common to both is the word, that is, the concept of Dyaus, or Greek Zeus, the sky as a person and as an agent. I may not always have spoken quite guardedly, and have taken certain things for granted which are understood by themselves among scholars. The important lesson is always the same. If Ahanâ is phonetically identical with Greek Athanâ and if Ahanâ is a name of the Dawn, it follows that the first conception of Athênê was the Dawn and that, as such, she sprang from the East or from the forehead of Zeus or Dyaus, the sky. If in the Veda she brings light and wakes and stirs up the thoughts of men, she became in Homer also the goddess of wisdom and the *τεχνῶν μήτηρ πολύολβος*. All this was perfectly known to Otfried Müller when in 1825 he wrote: "Because the name of the goddess was originally a word of the language and always remained so, Charis glided from poem to poem and preserved by means of the word her general meaning in every individual manifestation" (p. 249).

Sûn*ri*tâ, another name of the Dawn, is more difficult to explain. Sûn*ri*ta in the sense of true, seems to me to have been formed in mistaken analogy to An-*ri*ta *, untrue, and to have meant originally true, then sincere, gentle, agreeable. As applied to the Dawn it would have meant true, kind, auspicious.

But whatever obscurity there may still be left

* The two words are used together, as ubhayor antara*m* veda, sûn*ri*tân*ri*tayor api, Mahâbh. V, 5667.

as to the meaning of single words in our hymn, can any one doubt that the whole of it was simply an address or a prayer to the Dawn, without any reference, as yet, to any complicated ceremonial, as described in the Sûtras and Brâhma*n*as, and alluded to in some of the hymns also? And why this persistent searching for allusions to ceremonial? No one ever denied the presence of real allusions in the Vedic hymns. But it is a matter of degree, a question of more or less, and these ceremonial details, so far from proving our hymns to be very modern and the work of professed priests, serves only to prove, what was well known from other sources also, that savage or uncivilised races adhere at all times with great punctiliousness to their ceremonial customs and traditions. M. Bergaigne has done excellent work in pointing out traces of the same punctiliousness among Vedic poets, but he has allowed himself to be carried away much too far by his own system, without either paying sufficient attention to native commentaries or allowing sufficient credit to his predecessors, particularly in Germany. To speak of *ces philologues d'outre Rhin,* is entirely out of place in the republic of letters, and encourages a literary *chauvinisme* which will never find favour with the best scholars of France.

Leaving out Sûryâ, the female representative of

the sun, and more or less a Dawn again, and V*ri*shâkapâyî, because her character is not quite clear as yet, and Sara*n*yu=Erinys, because she is only mentioned in a few verses, we proceed now to Savit*ri*, the rising sun. Though Savit*ri* is a name applied to the sun in general, it is most frequently used as the name of the rising and life- and light-giving sun. Nor must it be supposed that Savit*ri* is simply an appellative of the solar globe. Savit*ri* has become a divine name or a divine *numen* as full of life and personality as any other Deva. He can therefore be asked, as he is in verse 9, to hale and bring back the real sun. We shall easily recognise his character in the following hymn (Rig-Veda I, 35, 2):—

HYMN TO SAVIT*RI*, SUN.

1.

I first call Agni * hither for our happiness,
I then call Mitra-Varu*n*a † to shield us here,
I call on Râtrî ‡, sending all the world to rest,
I call for help on Savit*ri*, the brightest god.

* Agni, fire, is here, as often, taken for the light of day.

† Mitra and Varu*n*a stand for morning and evening, or day and night.

‡ Râtrî, night, sometimes called the black day, K*ri*sh*n*am ahar, opposed to Ar*g*unam ahar, the bright day. Cf. Rig-Veda VI, 9, 1.

2.

Approaching on the darkest path of heaven,
Setting to rest both mortal and immortal,
God Savit*ri*, on golden chariot standing,
Comes hither and beholdeth all creation.

3.

The brilliant god moves upward and moves downward,
The worshipful, drawn by his brilliant racers,
And from afar god Savit*ri* approaches,
Driving away from us all that is evil *.

4.

God Savit*ri* stepped on his jewelled chariot,
The strong, the many-hued, its pins all golden †,
And he, the worshipful, in brightest splendour,
Displays his strength across the darkest welkin.

5.

Black with white hoofs the horses shone upon us,
Dragging along the golden-shafted chariot;
All men, all creatures here for ever rested,
Safe in the lap of Savit*ri* in heaven.

6.

Three skies are there of Savit*ri*, two places,
And one in Yama's realm that holds our heroes ‡,
Immortals § mounted on the chariot's axle,—
Let him speak out who understands this saying.

* Evil, physically darkness, morally sin.
† Pins of the chariot.
‡ The departed.
§ Explained as stars.

7.

The glorious bird* has lighted-up the heaven,
The guide divine, whose wings are deeply sounding;
Where is the sun? Who knows it now, to tell us,
Which of the heavens his ray may have illumined?

8.

The earth's eight quarters has the sun illumined,
Three miles of land, and all the seven rivers,
God Savit*r*i, the golden-eyed, has neared us,
And brought choice treasures to the liberal mortals.

9.

The golden Savit*r*i, who never rested,
Is moving forward, straight 'tween earth and heaven,
He strikes disease, and hales the sun from yonder;
Through darkest clouds up to the sky he hastens.

10.

The guide divine, with golden arms appearing,
May come to us, the rich and gracious giver,
Praised every night, the god did come towards us,
Chasing away the noxious evil spirits.

11.

O Savit*r*i, come hither on thy pathways,
The old, well-made ones, dustless in the heavens,
And on those paths be thou our sure protector,
And grant to us to-day thy gracious blessing!

* The sun.

Is there one verse in this hymn that is not perfectly clear and intelligible, as belonging to a hymn addressed to the personified deity of the sun? Let us once understand that Savit*ri* was a name of the sun, and why should he not be invoked for protection and for every kind of blessing? Of course, as soon as the sun was addressed by a poet, he ceased to be a mere sight. He became subjective, personal, and human, whether we like it or not. After that it does not require a great effort of imagination to address him as standing on a golden chariot, drawn by brilliant horses and all the rest. Surely the Vedic poets stood not alone in indulging in such imagery.

The sixth verse is no doubt difficult to understand in its minute detail, but its general sense is clear, and we must remember that the whole verse was really meant as a kind of riddle, a kind of amusement in which uncivilised races all over the world seem to have delighted.

Everything else is exactly what any poet might say of the sun. The sun might well be called a bird with golden wings, and if he is thanked for the treasures which he brings, surely the mere light of the morning and the warmth of the day are treasures sufficient for those whose very life must often have depended on the return of light and warmth after a cold and dark night, or on the return of spring after a severe winter. I cannot think that even native scholars could discover anything beyond what we ourselves see in this hymn, and as to M. Bergaigne, he must surely have been dazzled by his own system if he could perceive many, nay, any allusions to a highly developed system of sacrifice in any hymn like this. That such allusions exist in other hymns, I am very far from denying; what I deny is that liturgical thoughts ever obscured the broad physical features which formed the background of the ancient Vedic religion *, nay, of the Vedic ceremonial also, built up at first for the sake of regulating the times and seasons of the year. I am the very last to deny to M. Bergaigne and his pupils the merit of having made the sacrificial system of the Vedic hymns more intelligible, but they have not sufficiently resisted the temptation of trying the key that opened one drawer, on all the drawers that still remained to be unlocked.

These hymns would suffice for the gods of the morning, and may help to open the eyes of our mythological Parâv*rig*as, who cannot see the light because there is too much of it.

* Bergaigne, vol. ii., p. 277: "Les interprétations purement naturalistes, appliquées à l'analyse des mythes du Rig-Veda, laissent toujours, ou presque toujours, un résidu liturgique, et ce résidu, le plus souvent négligé jusqu'alors, en est précisément la partie la plus importante pour l'exégèse des hymnes."

I shall, however, add one more matutinal hymn addressed to Agni, not simply as the fire, but as the god of light which brightens the world every morning, and is in fact very difficult to distinguish from the sun. This Agni is sometimes called the first of all the gods. The word itself is the general name of fire in Sanskrit. It is phonetically the same as the Latin ignis, though the change of a into i is phonetically irregular. No one, however, is likely to be so bold an agnostic as to deny that the Âryas, before they separated, had made the discovery of fire, and given a name to it, such as Agni or ignis. What is most interesting in the development of this word is that while in India it entered into a very rich, religious, and mythological career, it remained a simple appellative in Italy, and was almost entirely lost and forgotten among the other Aryan nations. Should we be justified then in saying that the Latin ignis cannot possibly be the same word as Agni, because the latter is one of the greatest gods in the Veda, while ignis is no god at all? In the Veda Agni is a most prominent deity, though his character has often been misunderstood. Agni was, no doubt, the fire on the hearth and on the altar, and as such had his own development in India*. But Agni was also light in general, and more especially the light of

* See M. M., "Physical Religion," p. 120.

the sun, whether in the morning, or at noon, or in the evening. Thus we read, Rig-Veda III, 28, 1:—

> Agni, accept our offering, the cake, at the *morning libation!*
> Agni, eat the cake offered to thee when the *day is over!*
> Agni, accept here the cake at the *midday libation!*

Here Agni is clearly the sun, or the sunlight, or some power dwelling in the sun, all of which are very natural ideas with people in a nomadic or even agricultural state of society, nor do the three daily libations seem to me to point to any elaborate ceremonial. They are hardly more than the beginnings of the Sandhyâvandana and they could easily be matched among Semitic, nay, even among savage races.

In many hymns the solar character of Agni is merged in his domestic character, as the fire on the domestic hearth, as the centre of each family. Thus we read, Rig-Veda X, 1:—

HYMN TO AGNI.

1.

High*, at the head of Dawn, he stood, the mighty,
With light he came, emerging from the darkness,
Fair-bodied Agni with his radiant splendour
Has filled, when born, all human habitations.

* I have tried to preserve some of the Vedic rhythm in these translations, but I must apologise for these poetic efforts of

2.

Thou, being born, art child of Earth and Heaven,
Agni, the fair one, spread among the flowers * ;
The brilliant child by night and through the darkness,
Shouts for the cows † from far, above his mothers.

3.

Then knowing well the highest place in heaven,
As Vishnu, he, when born, protects the third place ‡.
And when their milk § has in his mouth been offered,
They sing to him with one accord their praises.

4.

And then the mothers, bringing food, approach him,
They bring him viands and they watch his increase ;
Though they have changed, thou goest again to see them
And art a priest ‖ among the tribes of mortals.

5.

Then hail to Agni, as the guest of mortals ‖,
The priest of holy rites on glittering chariot,
The brilliant signal ‖ of all sacrifices,
Of any god, by might divine, the equal.

mine in English. I have consulted, of course, the translations of Grassmann, Ludwig, Griffiths, and Bergaigne, and others where accessible, and have adopted some of the renderings which seemed to me particularly happy.

* Flowers and plants in general are supposed to be supported by warmth within them.

† The clouds that give their milk, the rain.

‡ The culminating point of the sun, between sunrise and sunset.

§ The milk of the clouds, or the rain.

‖ The fire on the hearth, in which oblations were offered.

6.

Then, dressed in raiment beautiful, and standing
In morning light, a priest on earth's old centre,
Thou, born in *Ilâ*'s place *, a king and high priest,
Shalt hither bring the gods to our oblation.

7.

For thou hast ever spread both earth and heaven †,
Again our friend, a true son to thy parents
Come hither, youthful god, to us who call thee,
And bring the gods, O son of strength ‡, to usward!

Now, I ask once more, can anything be more simple and natural? And can we not, without any great effort on our part, transport ourselves into the position of the Vedic poet who uttered these words, and follow his thoughts, as he gazed on the rising sun? No one would suppose that this poet was the first on earth who ever addressed the rising sun, and that it was he who coined all the names by which the sun is addressed in these short songs. We can easily see what a long distance lies behind him, behind his words and be-

* On the altar or the omphalos of the earth.

† Made visible.

‡ The rubbing of the fire-sticks required great strength and skill to bring out the fire that was supposed to be hidden in the wood. The fire, when lighted on the hearth, was supposed to bring the gods to their offerings; nay, by a change of cause and effect the fire kindled on the hearth was identified with the light kindled in the sky at the approach of the dawn.

hind his ideas. He was certainly not the first who invented priests and their sacrificial work. Only let us remember that, if we use such terms as priest or high priest, or king, we must not allow ourselves to assign to these terms, however unconsciously, all the meanings these words have with us.

These are very important cautions for people ignorant of Sanskrit, who have been led to imagine that the Vedic Âryas had kings like Solomon or Louis Quatorze, or High Priests like Samuel or Bossuet. The word which I translate by priest, is hot*ri*, which meant originally no more than shouter or invoker, and which in due time became the technical name of one of the sixteen *Ri*tvi*g*as or Season-priests. The other word Purohita means *praepositus*, or provost, and was at first no more than the priest who had to assist or to replace the father of a family, and had to see that all the offerings to the gods were made at the proper times and seasons, which probably was in the beginning no more than a contrivance for marking the essential divisions of the year.

Much depends here, as elsewhere, on the words which we use. Every act of worship may be called a sacrifice, and every sacred poet a high priest. To us these are very grand names and full of meaning. But let us look at some of the hymns addressed to Agni which are called sacrificial, and it seems to me that any peasant in his own cottage could have performed what is called a sacrifice, as presupposed, for instance, in the following hymn (Rig-Veda II, 6).

HYMN TO AGNI, FIRE.

Agni, accept this log of wood,
This service which I bring to thee,
Hear graciously these prayers and songs!

With this log let us honour thee,
Thou son of strength *, the horse's friend,
And with this hymn, thou nobly born.

And let us servants with our songs
Serve thee, the lover of our songs,
Wealth-lover, giver of our wealth!

Be thou our mighty, generous lord,
Thou lord and giver of our wealth,
And drive all hatred far from us!

He gives us rain from heaven above,
He gives unviolable strength,
He gives us food a thousandfold.

Come here, most youthful messenger,
To him who lauds and craves thy help,
Most holy priest †, called by our song.

* It required strength to rub out the sparks from the fire-sticks.

† The fire on the altar was supposed to call the gods, like a priest.

Agni, between both worlds *, O sage,
Thou passest, as a messenger
Between two hamlets, kind and wise,

Thou hast befriended us before,
Bring hither always all the gods,
And sit thou on this sacred turf †.

But whether these so-called sacrifices were in the beginning as complicated as they certainly were in the end, they are perfectly intelligible, and probably will become much more so when we know more of the literature in which they are described. How much of their development is presupposed in the Vedic hymns, I tried to explain, however shortly, as long ago as 1859 in my "History of Ancient Sanskrit Literature," p. 468, and much has been added by others during the last forty years; but when we speak of Vedic sacrifices, we must not think of the temple at Jerusalem, or of St. Peter's, but of a small plot of grass, on which a fire was kindled within the walls of piled up turf, and kept alive by pouring butter or fat upon it.

What is far more instructive in these hymns is the general attitude of the poet towards the sights of nature which attracted his attention, and the transition from a mere description of nature such as he saw it, to its being peopled with persons

* Heaven and earth, gods and men.
† The place where the fire was kept.

whom we call either divine or mythological. Here it is where the Veda has proved so useful, and has given quite a new character to the study of ancient religion and ancient mythology in every part of the world.

How much ingenuity was spent in former days to discover the origin of Zeus and the Greek dwellers on Olympus! After opening the Veda all becomes clear. What doubt can there remain that Zeus was Dyaus, originally the sky, but not the sky as the blue vault of heaven, but the sky as active, as personified and divine. We cannot expect to find many such cases as that of Dyaus = Zeus, where an Aryan god has preserved not only his old character in India and Greece and Italy, but his name, and that almost unchanged. We saw how the name of Agni was altogether lost in Greece, though preserved as an appellative in Italy. Yet the Greeks also had their god of fire, and their gods of light, such as Hephaestos, Apollon, Dionysos, Hermes and others, each developed in his own way. And here we come across some curious reminiscences among the Aryan nations. We saw how Agni, as morning sun, was called the son of heaven and earth. In other hymns he is actually called Dvimâtâ, having two mothers. This strange name meets us again in Greek Dimêtôr, in Latin as Bimatris. The child of two mothers or parents, a name quite intelligible, as we saw, in Sanskrit, as the son of heaven and earth, had become unintelligible in Greek and Latin, so that every kind of myth was invented to account for so strange a name. To say that the deity called Dvimâtâ in the Veda was the same as the Greek Dimêtôr or the Latin Bimatris would be going too far; but to say that Dimêtôr, i. e. Dionysos * was originally a god of light, as much as Agni, as much as Apollon and Hermes, the son of heaven and earth, is perfectly right and helps us to account for a number of myths in classical mythology.

These more hidden influences of ancient Aryan mythology on that of Greeks and Romans, are often the most interesting. We have a similar case in Jupiter Stator, which is generally explained as the stopper, stopping the soldiers from running away. That may be the Roman explanation, but in the Veda we have the same word Sthâtâ, applied to Indra, first as Sthâtâ harî*n*âm, i. e. holder of horses, when he comes in his chariot; then as Sthâtâ rathasya, holder or governor of the chariot. When this origin was once forgotten, it would be not unlikely that a new meaning was discovered in Stator, viz. the preserver of law and order, or the keeper in battle.

* Dyu-nisya.

If Agni, as in hymn X, 1, is identified with Vish*n*u, i. e. the sun in the zenith, we see how pliant the ideas of gods still were in the Veda. This Vish*n*u in India became in time as independent a deity as Apollon and Dionysos ever were in Greece, but they were all conceived as in the beginning sons of heaven and earth, and as closely allied with the sun in its various manifestations. The Vedic poet saw no difficulty in recognising the same elementary power in the sun rising in the morning, culminating at noon, and vanishing at night, nay in the fire on the hearth, and in the fire of the sacrifice, as the divine guest, the friend of the family, the priest on the altar. All this is not the Solar Theory, it is the Solar Fact, and not easily to be disposed of by an ignorant smile. Though Sanskrit scholars differ as much as other scholars, the broad facts of the Solar Theory have never been called in question by any competent authority, I mean, by anybody acquainted with Greek and Latin, and a little of Vedic Sanskrit.

While Agni here appears before us as the god of light in general, and often begins the procession of the daily gods as the light of the morning, as chasing away the dark night, as holding aloft the radiant sun, as leading forth the daughter of Dyaus (*Διὸς θυγάτηρ*) that is the Dawn, he being represented sometimes as the brother of the

Dawn, sometimes as her lover*, once even as kissing her†, there are other deities, equally representative of light, but more specialised in their functions. Sûrya himself, the Greek Helios, appears among the Vedic deities, and Ushas (Eos), the dawn, is called Sûrya-prabhâ or sunshine.

We have so far watched the daily procession of the Vedic gods as reflected in the hymns, beginning with Agni, as god of light, especially the light of the morning, and in many respects the *alter ego* of the sun. We saw that in one sense the Dawn also is only a female repetition of the auroral Agni (Agnir aushasya), and we met with a third personification of the morning sun in the shape of Savit*ri*, who is perhaps the most dramatic among the solar heroes, such as Mitra, Âditya, Vish*n*u and others.

The procession of the matutinal gods, which we have followed so far under the guidance of our old grammarian, Yâska, can be shown to rest on even earlier authority. Thus we read in one of the hymns themselves, Rig-Veda I, 157, 1:—

> Agni awoke, from earth arises Sûrya,
> Ushas, the great and bright, throws heaven open,
> The pair of Asvins yoked their car to travel,
> God Savit*ri* has roused the world to labour.

* X, 3, 3. † X, 4, 4.

There are other hymns, of course, that refer to the light of day or to the sun in his later stages also, culminating as Vish*n*u, or setting with T*r*ita, till at last Râtrî, night, appears and Varu*n*a, the coverer, reigns once more supreme in heaven. When we see Varu*n*a together with Mitra, the sun god, they represent a divine couple, dividing between them the sovereignty of the whole world, heaven and earth, very much like the A*s*vins. They are not so much in opposition to each other, as partners in a common work.

Just as the night, the sister of the Dawn, is sometimes conceived as a dawn or day (Ahan) herself, Mitra and Varu*n*a also seem often to be charged with the same duties. They hold heaven and earth asunder, they support heaven and earth and are the common guardians of the whole world. Varu*n*a as well as Mitra is represented as sun-eyed. Still the contrast between the two becomes gradually more and more pointed, and we can clearly see that, while light and day become the portion of Mitra, night and darkness fall more and more to the share of Varu*n*a. The sun is said to rise from the abode of Mitra and Varu*n*a, but night, moon, and stars are mentioned in the hymns already, as more closely related to Varu*n*a. Thus we read, Rig-Veda I, 27, 10:—

The stars fixed high in heaven and shining brightly
By night, O say, where have they gone by day-time?
The laws of Varu*n*a are everlasting,
The moon moves on by night in brilliant splendour.

In Rig-Veda VIII, 41, 10, we ought surely to translate, "He made the white-clothed black-clothed," and not, as proposed, "He made the black-clothed white-clothed," a change which is never ascribed to Varu*n*a.

This explains why some scholars went so far as to recognise in Varu*n*a the original representative of the moon or of the evening star, a far too narrow conception, however, of that supreme deity, though true, no doubt, so far as Varu*n*a, like the sky, comprehends within his sphere of influence night and stars as well as sun and dawn. The almost perfect identity of name between Varu*n*a and Ouranos shows that Varu*n*a was not only a Vedic or Indian deity, but had been named already in the Aryan period. There are phonetic difficulties, but how should we account for the coincidences in the name and character of these two gods?

These few specimens of Vedic poetry will suffice, I hope, to show what is meant by the Solar Theory. It means that most of the physical phenomena which impressed the mind of primitive races, like those that have left us their religious utterances in the Veda, were connected with the sun, with the light of the morning, with day and night succeeding each other, and regulating the whole life of an agricultural population. What else was there to interest such people and to draw away their thoughts from a visible to an invisible world? If I have sometimes called that population uncivilised, what I meant was that we come across customs, such as the selling of children or offering them as victims, polygamy, possibly even polyandry, which are generally considered as signs or survivals of savagery. Such general terms, however, are often very misleading, and because in the Râ*g*asûya sacrifice, for instance, there are remnants of disgusting customs, we must not allow ourselves to indulge with certain so-called missionaries in a general condemnation of the Vedic ceremonial. We should rather learn the lesson that ceremonial is generally the accumulation of centuries, and contains, besides much that may be useful, a large quantity of old rubbish, mostly misunderstood, muddled, and complicated, till the meaning of it, if it ever had any, is lost beyond the hope of recovery.

If anybody, after reading these few hymns, selected quite at random, can still doubt whether the Solar Theory is the only possible theory to account for these Vedic deities, and in consequence, for the Aryan deities connected with them by name or character, I have nothing more to say. I doubt the existence of such a person. He must in very truth be a solar myth. Let me say once more that I have never looked upon all Vedic deities as solar or matutinal, but that other physical phenomena also, such as rivers, clouds, earth, night, storms, and rain had been personified or deified before these hymns could have been composed. It is true there is one hymn only addressed exclusively to the Night (X, 127), two only addressed to the Earth, but I pointed out before why such statistics, though very tempting, are altogether untrustworthy and have nothing whatever to do with the real importance or popularity of these deities. Does the ninth Ma*nd*ala of the Rig-Veda, with its 114 hymns almost entirely addressed to Soma, prove the supreme popularity of Soma as a member of the Vedic Pantheon? However, to guard against all possibility of misapprehending my purpose, here follows the hymn to Râtrî or Night; which can hardly be called solar in the usual sense of that word.

HYMN TO RÂTRÎ, NIGHT.

1.

The Night comes near and looks about,
The goddess with her many eyes,
She has put on her glories all.

2.

Immortal, she has filled the space,
Both far and wide, both low and high,
She conquers darkness with her light*.

3.

She has undone her sister, Dawn†,
The goddess Night, as she approached,
And utter darkness ‡ flies away.

4.

For thou art she in whose approach
We seek to-day for rest, like birds
Who in the branches seek their nest.

5.

The villages have sought for rest,
And all that walks and all that flies,
The falcons come, intent on prey.

6.

Keep off the she-wolf, keep the wolf,
Keep off the thief, O kindly Night,
And be thou light for us to pass.

7.

Black darkness came, yet bright with stars,
It came to us, with brilliant hues ;
Dawn, free us as from heavy debt!

* The darkness of the night is lighted by the light of the moon and stars.

† The dawn or bright day that lasts from morning till evening.

‡ The darkness caused by the retreat of Dawn or Day, is lighted up by the brilliant Night.

8.

Like cows, I brought this hymn to thee,
As to a conqueror, child of Dyaus,
Accept it graciously, O Night!

We must remember that the night to the Vedic poet was not the same as darkness, but that on the contrary, when the night had driven away the day, she was supposed to lighten the darkness, and even to rival her sister, the bright day, with her starlight beauty. The night, no doubt, gives peace and rest, yet the Dawn is looked upon as the kindlier light, and is implored to free mortals from the dangers of the night, as debtors are freed from a debt. Many conjectural alterations have been proposed in this hymn, but it seems to me to be intelligible even as it stands.

One more hymn to show how the belief in and the worship of these physical gods, the actors behind the phenomena of nature, could grow naturally into a belief in and a worship of moral powers, endowed with all the qualities essential to divine beings. Moral ideas are not so entirely absent from the Veda, as has sometimes been asserted, and nothing can be more instructive than to watch the process by which they spring naturally from a belief in the gods of nature. I give the hymn to Varu*n*a from Rig-Veda VII, 86, which I translated for the first time in my "History of Ancient Sanskrit Literature" in the year 1859, and which, with the help of other translations published in the mean time, I have now tried to improve and to clothe in the metrical form of the original.

HYMN TO VARU*N*A.

1.

Wise, surely, through his might is his creation,
Who stemmed asunder spacious earth and heaven;
He pushed the sky, the bright and glorious, upward,
And stretched the starry sky and earth asunder.

2.

With my own heart I commune, how I ever
Can now approach Varu*n*a's sacred presence;
Will he accept my gift without displeasure?
When may I fearless look and find him gracious?

3.

Fain to discover this my sin, I question,
I go to those who know, and ask for counsel.
The same reply I get from all the sages,
'Tis Varu*n*a indeed whom thou hast angered.

4.

What was my chief offence that thou wilt slay me,
Thy oldest friend who always sang thy praises?
Tell me, unconquered Lord, and I shall quickly
Fall down before thee, sinless with my homage.

5.

Loose us from sins committed by our fathers,
From others too which we ourselves committed,
As from a calf, take from us all our fetters,
Loose us as thieves are loosed that lifted cattle.

6.

'Twas not our own free will, 'twas strong temptation,
Or thoughtlessness, strong drink, or dice, or passion,
The old was near to lead astray the younger,
Nay, sleep itself suggests unrighteous actions.

7.

Let me do service to the bounteous giver,
The angry god, like to a slave, but sinless;
The gracious god gave wisdom to the foolish,
And he, the wiser, leads the wise to riches.

8.

O let this song, god Varu*n*a, approach thee,
And let it reach thy heart, O Lord and Master!
Prosper thou us in winning and in keeping,
Protect us, gods, for evermore with blessings!

I wish I could have introduced a larger number of my so-called Indian friends, the poets of sacred songs who may have lived thousands of years ago. But I am afraid I have already tired out the patience of my readers with these very ancient friends of mine. The only excuse I can plead is that my own friends in England and in Germany have so often wondered how I could have fallen in love with the Veda, and actually left my own country in order to rescue this forgotten Bible from utter oblivion. It is fortunate that people have different tastes and that we are not all devoted to the same beauty.

One more hymn I must add, however, for I am afraid if I do not, I shall be accused of having misrepresented the character of the Veda, as reflecting only the simplest thoughts of shepherds and cultivators of the land. I have remarked several times before that the Rig-Veda contains some very striking philosophical passages, and how far some of the Vedic poets must have been carried by purely metaphysical speculations may be seen by a hymn which I translated for the first time in my "History of Ancient Sanskrit Literature," 1859. In putting it into a metrical form I was helped at the time by my departed friend, the late Archbishop of York, then Mr. Thomson, and I am glad to say I find little to alter in his translation even now.

HYMN X, 129.

Nor aught nor naught existed; yon bright sky
Was not, nor heaven's broad woof outstretched above;
What covered all? what sheltered? what concealed?
Was it the waters' fathomless abyss?
There was not death, hence was there naught immortal,

There was no light of night, no light of day,
The only One breathed breathless in itself,
Other than it there nothing since has been.
Darkness there was, and all at first was veiled
In gloom profound, an ocean without light;
The germ that still lay covered in the husk,
Burst forth, one nature, from the fervent heat.
Then first came Love upon it, the new germ,
Of mind; yea, poets in their hearts discerned
Pondering this bond between created things
And uncreated. Came this ray from earth
Piercing and all-pervading, or from heaven?
Then seeds were sown, and mighty powers arose,
Nature below, and Power and Will above;
Who knows the secret? who proclaimed it here,
Whence, whence this manifold creation sprang?
The gods themselves came later into being,
Who knows from whence this great creation sprang?
He from whom all this great creation came,
Whether his will created or was mute,
The most high Seer that is in highest heaven,
He knows it—or perchance e'en He knows not.

This hymn is important, not only by what it says, but by what it presupposes. Whatever date we may ascribe to it as incorporated in the Rig-Veda, many generations of thinkers must have passed before such questions could have been asked or could have been answered. As yet we see the Vedic age only as through a glass darkly. The first generation of Vedic scholars is passing away. It has done its work bravely, though well aware of its limits. Let the next generation dig deeper and deeper. What is wanted is patient, but independent and original work. There is so much new ground still to be broken, that the time has hardly come as yet for going again and again over the same ploughed field.

I must now part with my Vedic Friends. I can hardly hope that I have persuaded many of my English friends to share my feelings for my antediluvian acquaintances. All I care for is to make others understand how my heart was caught, and what I saw in my Indian love, not only in her Vedântic dreams and aspirations, but in the simplicity of her earliest utterances of trust in powers invisible, yèt present behind what is visible, and in her faith in a law that rules both the natural and the supernatural world.

MY INDIAN FRIENDS

V

A PRIME MINISTER AND A CHILD-WIFE

I HAVE often had to give expression to a certain disappointment at not being able, when speaking of my Indian friends, to reveal more of their inner life. That life, we may be certain, is not absent, but it is kept hidden, just as Indian women are kept behind their purdahs or curtains and hidden under veils, more or less transparent. Some of our own distinguished men and women are perhaps too much given to perform their confessions and moral ablutions in public, while in India such books as Rousseau's *Confessions*, or the *Confessions of St. Augustine*, nay, of Amiel or Marie Bashkirtseff, to mention some well-known instances only, can hardly be imagined. Introspection or self-examination exists no doubt among the men and women of India as well as anywhere else. But unless such inward searchings take a definite form in words, nay, in written and published words, they can hardly be said to exist. A man may enter into a dark cave and see visions, but unless he can find his way back into the bright light of day, unless he can find words for what was vaguely passing through the twilight of his memory, all vanishes again and leaves nothing behind but a nameless sentiment, like the feeling that is left by a dream, when we know indeed that we have been dreaming, but cannot recall what we saw in our dreams.

Even in the prayers which we possess of the people in India we find no very deep delvings into the soul of man. They consist chiefly of praises of the greatness of the gods or of God, of general confessions of human weakness or sin, but we hardly ever come across the agonised sufferings of self-reproachful saints, and we see little of that moral vivisection which, painful as it is to witness, often reveals to us some of the most secret springs of human nature which nothing else will bring to our view.

I cannot, therefore, even in the two cases of Indian friends which I have selected for my purpose here, promise anything like that minute moral and spiritual analysis which we find in the works of St. Augustine, of Rousseau, or Marie Bashkirtseff. One of my friends belonged to the highest, the other to the lowest ranks of Indian life; the one was a Prime Minister, the other what we should call a poor peasant-girl. I was brought into contact with them, not indeed face to face, but by correspondence only. The Prime Minister was the well-known Gaurîshankar Udayshankar Ozá, Minister of Bhavnagar. I am afraid that when people see these long and unpronounceable names they will at once put down the book. Names such as Rudyard Kipling, Bashkirtseff, or Pobedonostzeff may be mastered in time, but Gaurîshankar Udayshankar Ozá is too much for most people's memories; and how can people, even if they manage to pronounce such a name, attach any meaning whatever to it? It might be better, perhaps, to give the name in its Sanskrit form, viz. Gaurî-*s*ankara; we could then see some kind of meaning in it, provided we knew a little of Sanskrit. So far as one may guess the meaning of any proper names, Gaurî-*s*ankara would be the name of the divine couple, *S*iva, sometimes called *S*ankara, and Gaurî, better known under the name of Pârvatî, his wife. Of course the name may be interpreted differently also, but when we know that Gaurî stands for Pârvatî, and Shankar for *S*iva, we move at once in more or less familiar spheres, and we may look on the name as something like the Christian name Joseph Maria, which is not unusual as a Christian name in Roman Catholic countries. But when I call Gaurî-*s*ankara the well-known Prime Minister of Bhavnagar, I anticipate another shrugging of the shoulders. What is Bhavnagar, where is it, and what is there really known about its "well-known" Prime Minister? Here are our difficulties, when we want to rouse the sympathies of our readers for anything connected with India. Yes, if Gaurî-*s*ankara of Bhavnagar were Fergus McIvor, chief of Glennaquoich, all would go well. But to most people, except those who have been in India, Bhavnagar is almost a *terra incognita*, and as there are now no separate postage-stamps for the independent states of India, even children would say that there is no such state as Bhavnagar anywhere. Still there is a native state of that name in Kathiawar, with about 500,000 inhabitants, and there is a Râjah, who is called the Thakur Sahib of Bhavnagar. There is also a town of Bhavnagar, the capital of the state. Like most of the protected Rajput states, Bhavnagar enjoys as much freedom as is compatible with the welfare of its neighbours and the imperial interests of India. Under such conditions conflicts are, no doubt, inevitable, and it required no little statesmanship in the Râjah, and in his Dewân, or Prime Minister, to reconcile the interests of their subjects with those of their neighbours and with those of the British Empire. Quite a new class of native statesmen seems to have sprung up of late in these various dependent states, who are enabled, through the moral support which they receive from the Central Government, to reform the abuses of a personal and autocratic *régime*, to revive education, and to improve the sanitary condition of the towns and villages, to open commercial communications, and altogether to raise the political and moral status and character of the people committed to their charge. In many cases they had at the same time to keep on good terms with the English residents, who are not always the most amiable, and to protect the Râjahs themselves against the corrupting influences of their little courts and harems. Taking all this together, it is not difficult to see that their position was by no means an easy one, and that it required high qualities indeed in these native statesmen to enable them to hold their own, to satisfy the claims of all the parties with whom they had to deal, and at the same time not to stifle the voice of their own conscience.

But when an opening had once been made for native talent in this direction, native talent was not wanting. The names of such men as Sir Salar Jung in Hyderabad, Sir T. Madao Rao in Travancore, Indore, and Baroda, Sir Dinkar Rao in Gwalior, are well known, not in India only, but in England also, and not the least successful among them was our friend Gaurî-*s*ankara.

With all the narrow prejudices of Oriental society, particularly in India, there was always *a carrière ouverte aux talents.* Gaurî-*s*ankara was the son of a poor man, though he belonged to a good Brâhmanic family. His education would not, perhaps, have enabled him to pass the Indian Civil Service Examination, and yet what an excellent Civil servant would he have made. Examinations prevent many evils, but they cannot create or even discover the qualities necessary for a ruler of men.

Like Mr. Gladstone, Gaurî-*s*ankara became known in India as the Grand Old Man, or, better still, as the Good Old Man, and, like Mr. Gladstone, he represented in himself a striking combination of the thinker and the doer, of the meditative and the active man. His deepest interest lay with the great problems of human life on earth, but this did not prevent him from taking a most active part in the great and small concerns of the daily life and the daily cares of a small state. He acted as Minister to four generations of the rulers of Bhavnagar, and he was a constant referee on intricate political questions to successive Political agents of Kathiawar. He could remember the first establishment of British authority in the Bombay Presidency, and he had been the contemporary and fellow-worker of Mountstuart Elphinstone at the time when the settlement of Guzarat and Kathiawar had to be worked out between the Gaikwar on one side and the English Government, as successor of the Peshwa, on the other. He came in contact not only with Mountstuart Elphinstone, who visited Kathiawar in 1821, but with Sir John Malcolm also, with Lord Elphinstone and Sir Bartle Frere—nay, as late as 1886, with Lord Reay, then Governor of the Bombay Presidency. After a conference with the old man—he was then eighty-one years of age, having been born in 1805—Lord Reay declared that he was struck as much by the clearness of his intellect as by the simplicity and fairness and openness of his mind; "and if we admire administrators," he added, "we also admire straightforward advisers—those who tell their chiefs the real truth about the condition of their country and their subjects. In seeing the man who freed this State from all incumbrances, who restored civil and criminal jurisdiction to their villages, who settled grave disputes with Junaghad, who got rid of refractory Jemadars, I could not help thinking what could be done by such men of purpose and strength of character."

These words contain a rapid survey of the work of a whole life, and if we were to enter here into the details of what was actually achieved by this native statesman we should find that few Prime Ministers even of the greatest states in Europe had so many tasks on their hands, and performed them so boldly and so well. The clock on the tower of the Houses of Parliament strikes louder than the repeater in our waistcoat pocket, but the machinery, the wheels within wheels, and particularly the spring, have all the same tasks to perform as in Big Ben himself. Even men like Disraeli or Gladstone, if placed in the position of these native statesmen, could hardly have been more successful in grappling with the difficulties of a new state, with rebellious subjects, envious neighbours, a weak sovereign, and an all-powerful suzerain, to say nothing of court intrigues, religious squabbles, and corrupt officials. We are too much given to measure the capacity of ministers and statesmen by the magnitude of the results which they achieve with the immense forces placed at their disposal. But most of them are very ordinary mortals, and it is not too much to say that for making a successful marriage-settlement a country solicitor stands often in need of the same vigilance, the same knowledge of men and women, the same tact, and the same determination or bluff which Bismarck displayed in making the treaty of Prague or of Frankfurt. Nay, there are mistakes made by the greatest statesmen in history which, if made by our solicitor, would lead to his instant dismissal. If Bismarck made

Germany, Gaurî-*s*ankara made Bhavnagar. The two achievements are so different that even to compare them seems absurd, but the methods to be followed in either case are, after all, the same; nay, it is well known that the making or regulating of a small watch may require more nimble and careful fingers than the large clock of a cathedral. We are so apt to imagine that the man who performs a great work is a great man, though from revelations lately made we ought to have learnt how small—nay, how mean—some of these so-called great men have really been.

Gaurî-*s*ankara found nothing to begin with—or rather, less than nothing, for he found not only an unorganised but a disorganised state. General Keatinge, who was Political Agent of Kathiawar during the years 1863 to 1867, found the transformation that had been wrought by Gaurî-*s*ankara so complete that he could hardly believe that Bhavnagar was the same town which he had known in former days. Splendid buildings had arisen, devoted either to education or to the relief of the sick, the poor, and the needy. The harbour had been improved, and roads for trade and communications of every kind had been newly laid out or made serviceable. There was a large reservoir to supply the town with water; there were paddocks, a new jail, two medical dispensaries, and an immense hospital; there were telegraph and post offices, a High School, and a High Court of Justice. A railway had been built from Bhavnagar to Gondal, and so well was it administered, without syndicates or any other kind of jobbery, that it yielded annually a fair revenue to the state. The responsibility for all these undertakings rested on the shoulders of one man, and the credit for them should rest there also.

All this, however, is not what interested me in the old man, nor will it, I fear, interest many of my readers. He is after all but one of the many unknown ants that build up hills which, for all we know, one stroke of a stick may destroy again. Nor was it his moral character, noble and pure as it doubtless must have been, that riveted my attention chiefly. A man could hardly have achieved what he did, unless he stood high above the reach of the vulgar vices and failings of mankind. In that direction, I may quote a few more judgments from the mouths of those who had known him during his long active life. "His chief strength," as one of his friends writes, "was to be found in his exemplary private character—

"His words were bonds, his oaths were oracles,
His love sincere, his thoughts immaculate;
His tears pure messengers sent from his heart;
His heart as far from fraud as heaven from earth."

This is beautifully expressed; but does it give us an image of the man himself? Even the strongest words seem so colourless when they are meant to give us the picture of a living man. It may be quite true that he enjoyed in private and domestic life a veneration that was due to his noble and patriarchal character, and that his influence was, as we are told, invariably and unerringly exerted in putting an extinguisher on private feuds and disagreements among a wide and ever-widening circle of relations, friends, and members of his caste. We read that "in order to promote harmony among them he often made personal sacrifices, and that he proved himself a friend of the needy and the helpless, of genius and talent struggling to rise. If it was not to be a blessing to others, life seemed to him not worth living."

All this is very strong testimony; and yet of how many people has the same been said, particularly by mourners at the grave of one whom they loved, and who had loved them! Funeral eloquence has its bright, but it also has its very dark side. It is delightful to see how much can be forgotten and forgiven at the grave, how gently all faults can be passed over or accounted for, how none but the noblest motives can then be imputed. But all is spoiled at once if rhetorical exaggeration comes in, so that even the truth contained in the panegyrics is hidden and choked by a rank growth of adulation and untruthfulness.

But though I was quite prepared to believe all that we were told about the private as well as public character of Gaurî-sankara, what attracted me most in him was that the same man should through life have been a true philosopher, nay, what men of the world would call a dreamer of dreams; and should yet have proved so excellent a man of business. Plato's dictum, which has so often been ridiculed, that philosophers are the true rulers of men, has indeed been signally vindicated in Gaurî-sankara's case. And his philosophy was not what may be called useful philosophy—a knowledge of nature and its laws. This might be tolerated in a Prime Minister, even in Europe. No; it consisted in the most abstruse metaphysics which would turn even the hardened brains of some of our best philosophers perfectly giddy. And yet that very philosophy, so far from unfitting Gaurî-sankara for his arduous work, gave him the proper strength for doing and doing well whatever from day to day his hands found to do. He felt the importance of his official work to the fullest extent, but he always felt that there was something more important still. Though devoting all his powers to this life and its duties, he felt convinced that this life would soon pass away, that there was no true reality in it, that it was Mâyâ, illusion, arising from Avidyâ, nescience, and that there was behind, beneath, and above, another and higher life which alone was worth living. It was his faith in, or his knowledge of, that higher life which best fitted him to perform his work in the turmoil of the world. Thus it was that when any of his schemes ended in failure, disappointment never upset him, and that though he was often deceived in the friends he had trusted, he never became a pessimist.

It is very difficult to describe what was the faith or the philosophy which supported him throughout his busy life. From his early youth he was impressed with certain views of the Vedânta philosophy, which form the common spiritual property, so to say, of all the inhabitants of India. That philosophy seems to have entered into the very life-blood of the nation, but it assumed, of course, very different forms as believed in by men of talent and education, and by the drudging tillers of the soil throughout the land. The number of those who study the Vedânta in the works of such minute philosophers as Bâdarâya*n*a and *S*ankara is naturally very small, but the number of those who have drunk in the spirit of it, it may be in a few sayings only, is legion.

It seems almost impossible to give a short and clear account of that ancient philosophy, though, when once known, it can be, and has been, described and epitomised in a few very short lines. The approaches to it are very various, but anybody accustomed to Greek or European forms of thought is sorely perplexed how to find an entrance into it from exactly the same point as the Hindus themselves. The Vedânta philosophy is meant to be an interpretation of the world, different from all other interpretations, whether philosophical or religious. It was to lead to a new birth, and therefore remained unintelligible and unmeaning to souls that will not be regenerated. It is partly an advantage, partly a disadvantage, that for several of their most important tenets the Vedântists simply appeal to the Vedas, their Bible, as containing the absolute truth, as being the highest seat of authority, or the last Court of Appeal on questions which with us would require very different arguments to prove that, given our reasoning powers, such as they are, and the world, such as it is, certain doctrines are inevitable, or that at all events their opposites are unthinkable. To make the results at which the Vedântists arrive intelligible, it is best for us to start with a few maxims which seem to underlie their philosophy, and which, whether true in themselves or not, do not at all events offend against our own rules of reasoning.

If, then, we start with the idea of the Godhead, which is never quite absent in any system of philosophy or religion, we may, excluding all polytheistic forms of faith, allow our friends, the Vedântists, to lay it down that before all things the Godhead must be one, so that it may not be limited or conditioned by anything else. This is the Vedânta tenet which they express by the ever-recurring formula that the Sat, the true Being or Brahman, must be Ekam, one, and Advitîyam, without any second whatsoever. If, then, it is once admitted that in the beginning, in the present, and in the future, the Godhead must be one, all, and everything, it follows that nothing but that Godhead can be conceived as the true, though distant cause of everything material as well as spiritual, of our body as well as of our soul. Another maxim of the Vedântist, which likewise could hardly be gainsaid by any thinker, is that the Godhead, if it exists at all in its postulated character, must be unchangeable, because it is perfect and cannot possibly be interfered with by anything else, there being nothing beside itself. On this point also all the advanced religions seem agreed. But then arises at once the next question, If the Godhead is one without a second, and if it is unchangeable, whence comes change or development into the world; nay, whence comes the world itself, or what we call creation—whence comes nature with its ever-changing life and growth and decay?

Here the Vedântist answer sounds at first very strange to us, and yet it is not so very different from other philosophies. The Vedântist evidently holds, though this view is implied rather than enunciated, that, as far as we are concerned, the objective world is, and can only be, *our knowledge* of the objective world, and that everything that is objective is *ipso facto* phenomenal. Objective, if properly analysed, is to the Vedântist the same as phenomenal, the result of what *we* see, hear, and touch. Nothing objective could exist objectively, except as perceived by us, nor can we ever go beyond this, and come nearer in any other way to the hidden, subjective part of the objective world, to the *Ding an sich* supposed to be without us. If, then, we perceive that the objective world—that is, whatever we know by our senses, call it nature or anything else—is always changing, whilst on the other hand, the one Being that exists, the Sat, can be one only, without a second, and without change, the only way to escape from this dilemma is to take the world when known to us as purely phenomenal, i. e. as created by our knowledge of it, only that what we call knowledge is called from a higher point of view not knowledge, but Avidyâ, i. e., Nescience. Thus the Godhead, though being that which alone supplies the reality underlying the objective world, is never itself objective, still less can it be changing. This is illustrated by a simile, such as are frequently used by the Vedântists, not to prove a thing, but to make things clear and intelligible. When the sun is reflected in the running water it seems to move and to change, but in reality it remains unaffected and unchanged. What our senses see is phenomenal, but it evidences a reality sustaining it. It is, therefore, not false or illusory, but it is phenomenal. It is fully recognised that there could not be even a phenomenal world without that postulated real Sat, that power which we call the Godhead, as distinguished from God or the gods, which are its phenomenal manifestations, known to us under different names.

The Sat, or the cause remains itself, always one and the same, unknowable and nameless. And what applies to external nature applies likewise to whatever name we may give to our internal, eternal, or subjective nature. Our true being—call it soul, or mind, or anything else—is the Sat, the Godhead, and nothing else, and that is what the Vedântists call the Self or the Âtman. That

Âtman, however, as soon as it looks upon itself, becomes *ipso facto* phenomenal, at least for a time; it becomes the I, and that I may change. The I is not one, but many. It is the Âtman in a state of Nescience, but when that Nescience is removed by Vidyâ, or philosophy, the phenomenal I vanishes in death, or even before death, and becomes what it always has been, Âtman, which Âtman is nothing but the Sat, the Brahman, or, in our language, the Godhead.

These ideas, though not exactly in this form or in this succession, seem to me to underlie all Vedântic philosophy, and they will, at all events, form the best and easiest introduction to its sanctuary. And, strange as some of these ideas may sound to us, they are really not so very far removed from the earlier doctrines of Christianity. The belief in a Godhead beyond the Divine Persons is clearly enunciated in the much-abused Athanasian Creed, of which in my heart of hearts I often feel inclined to say: "Except a man believe it faithfully, he cannot be saved." There is but one step which the Vedântists would seem inclined to take beyond us. The Second Person, or what the earliest Christians called the Word—that is, the divine idea of the universe, culminating in the highest concept, the Logos of Man—would be with them the *Thou*, i. e., the created world. And while the early Christians saw that divine ideal of manhood realised and incarnate in one historical person, the Vedântist would probably not go beyond recognising that highest Logos, the Son of God and the Son of man, as Man, as every man, whose manhood, springing from the Godhead, must be taken back into the Godhead. And here is the point where the Vedântist differs from all other so-called mystic religions which have as their highest object the approach of the soul to God, the union of the two, or the absorption of the one into the other. The Vedântist does not admit any such approach or union between God and man, but only a recovery of man's true nature, a remembrance or restoration of his divine nature or of his godhead, which has always been there, though covered for a time by Nescience. After this point has once been reached, there would be no great difficulty in bringing on an agreement between Christianity, such as it was in its original form, and Vedântism, the religious philosophy of India. What seems to us almost blasphemy—a kind of *apotheosis* of man, is with the Vedântist an act of the highest reverence. It is taken as man's *anatheosis*, or return to his true Father, a recovery of his true godlike nature. And what is or can be the meaning of God-like? Can anything be godlike that is not originally divine, though hidden for a time by

Nescience? After all, though Nescience may represent Manhood as the very opposite of Godhead, what beings are there, or can be imagined to be, that could fill the artificial interval that has been established long ago between God and man, unless we allow our poets to people that interval with angels and devils? The real difficulty is how that interval, that abyss between God and man, was ever created, and if the Vedântist says by Nescience, is that so different from what we say "By human ignorance."

It was necessary to give these somewhat abstruse explanations—though in reality they are not abstruse, but intelligible to every unsophisticated and childlike mind. These, then, were the ideas that supported our friend Gaurî-*s*ankara, and which support, under different disguises, millions of human beings in India—men, women, and children. On such simple but solid foundations it is easy to erect ever so many religions, to build ever so many temples, and to find room for the most elevated and the most superstitious minds, all yearning for the same Peace of God, and for the same Giver of Peace and Rest. Names may differ and truth may adopt different disguises. But, after all, the peace which Gaurî-*s*ankara enjoyed amid the daily cares of his official life, and which arose from his forgetting himself and finding himself in

God, or, as he would say, forgetting his phenomenal in his real Âtman, could it have been so very different from what we call the peace of God that passes all understanding? Such a view of the world as his was, is generally supposed to unfit a man for all practical work, but this, as we see, is by no means a necessary consequence. One thought of Brahman was sufficient to refresh and strengthen him for the battle of life, like a header taken into the waves of an unfathomable ocean. He knew where he was and what he was, and that was enough to keep him afloat.

And here we come across another curious feature of Hindu life, which shows how thoroughly their philosophy had leavened and shaped their social institutions in ancient times. As soon as we know anything of these institutions we read that the passage through life of a twice-born man was divided into four periods—one of the pupil, Brahma*k*ârin, the next of the married man or the householder, G*ri*hastha. Then followed the third stage, after a man had fulfilled all his duties, had performed all necessary sacrifices, and had seen the children of his children. Then and then only came the time when he might retire from his house, give up all that belonged to him, and settle somewhere in the forest near, with or without his wife, but still accessible to his relations, and chiefly occupied in overcoming all passions by means of ascetic exercises, and withdrawing his affections more and more from all the things of this life. During that third station, that of the Vânaprastha or the ὑλόβιος, the mind of the hermit became more and more concentrated on that higher philosophy which we call religion, and more particularly on the Vedânta, as contained in the Upanishads, and similar but later works. Instead of merely dipping into the waters, the philosophical baptism became then a complete submergence, an entrance into life with Brahman, where alone perfect peace and a perfect satisfaction of man's spiritual desires could be found. This third station was followed by a fourth—the last chapter of life, when the old and decrepit man dragged himself away into the deep solitude of the forest, forgetting all that had once troubled or delighted his heart, and falling at last into the arms of his last friend, Death.

Such a conception and division of life seems quite natural from a Hindu point of view, and there was no necessity therefore for explaining it, as some anthropologists have done, by a circuitous appeal to savage customs, as is now the fashion. It is well-known, no doubt, that both savage and half-civilised races get rid of their old people by either killing them or by causing them to be killed by wild animals. This inhuman cruelty may, no doubt, have been an act of necessity, particularly during a nomadic state of life. But in India the third station of life is quite different. It is based on a voluntary act, and it is followed by a fourth and final station, equally chosen by a man's own free will. Besides, all this was meant for the higher classes only, without a hint of its ever having been considered as inhuman or cruel. These anthropological explanations are very amusing, no doubt; their only drawback is that most of them can neither be proved nor disproved.

At present the four stations of life in India seem to possess an archaeological interest only, they are no longer of any practical importance. In the case of Gaurî-*s*ankara it was no doubt his love of the ancient customs of his country, combined with a true desire for rest at the end of a most laborious and most successful career, that made him think of reviving in his own case the old custom, though even then in a milder form only. He gave up his post as Prime Minister, and entered into private life in January, 1879. His mind, we are told, when he was bordering upon eighty, was as bright and active as ever, but he then directed all his mental energies to one subject only, to a constant contemplation of the great problems of life. His presence had attracted many itinerant anchorites, many eminent teachers and students of the Vedânta to Bhavnagar, which became for a time the home of Indian philosophical speculation. He himself now devoted his time to a serious study of Sanskrit, for which his incessantly busy career had left him little time in youth. He published in 1884 *The Svarûpânusandhâna* in Sanskrit, being considerations on the nature of the Âtmâ (Self), and on the unity of the Âtmâ with the Paramâtmâ (the Highest Self). He still saw some friends, and, living in what we should call a garden house, he remained in touch with the outer world, though no longer affected by any of the conflicting interests which had occupied him for so many years. When, in 1886, Lord and Lady Reay wished to see him once more, he consented to receive them, but in the dress, or rather uniform, of his Order, with his Dhoti, his frock, and his cap all covered with ochre. Their interview lasted for an hour, and Lord Reay declared that of all the happy moments he spent in India, those spent in the presence of that remarkable man remained engraved on his memory.

A few letters which I received from the old man after his retirement from the world may be interesting. He had sent me a copy of his book which contained, as he said, a collection of Vedântic sentences, forming, as it were, a chain of precious jewels or pearls. I thanked him in the same spirit, and as my letter has been published in his Life, I may as well repeat it here:—

OXFORD, *December* 3, 1884.

I have to thank you for your kind letter and for your valuable present, the Svarûpânusandhâna. If you had sent me a real necklace of precious stones it might have been called a magnificent present, but it would not have benefited myself, my true Âtman. The necklace of precious sentences which you have sent me has, however, benefited myself, my true Âtman, and I, therefore, consider it a far more precious present than mere stones or pearls. Besides, in accepting it, I need not be ashamed, for they become only my own, if I deserve them, that is, if I truly understand them. While we are still in our first and second Âsrama (station of life) we cannot help differing from one another according to the country in which we are born, according to the language we speak, and according to the Dharma (religion) in which we have been educated. But when we enter into the third and fourth Âsrama, into which you have entered and I am entering, we differ no longer, *Gn*âtvâ Deva*m* sarvapâsâpahâni*h*: "When God has become really known, all fetters fall."

Though in this life we shall never meet, I am glad to have met you in spirit.

I received another letter from him when he was just on the point of retiring from the world altogether and becoming a Sannyâsin, as far as that is possible in modern India. By taking this step he showed that he was indeed a Vedântist in good earnest. What with us is but one of the many theories of life, was to him the only saving faith; and while with us an old Prime Minister clings to the end to his political interests, and loves to be surrounded and amused by those who belong to him, we see here a real hero of thought who, freed from all desires, turns his eyes away from the whole phenomenal world to dwell only on what is eternal and unchangeable, the Paramâtman—the Highest Self. To most of us this intellectual atmosphere, which he breathed to the very last, would prove too exhausting. We can never drop all fetters—nay, many of us glory in them to the very end. But whatever we may think of his philosophy, there can be no doubt that his life was consistent throughout. He tried to live up to the standard which had been handed down to him from remote antiquity, and which he fully believed to be the best and the truest. This last letter is dated July 11, 1886. In it he says:—

I had sent you a book which is the result of my long study of the Vedânta Philosophy. You can easily imagine that I, being a Hindu Brâhman, can be said to have fully realised the truth of the doctrine therein discussed, when I can give you patent proofs of the effect which that study has had on me. There are, as you well know, four Âsramas prescribed by our *S*âstras, and the Brâhmans are required to successively pass through them all, if they can do so. But in this Kaliyuga people are not very particular about it. The second Âsrama, namely that of G*ri*hastha (householder), is more or less enjoyed by all, and there are some who enter into the third or fourth order. Fortunately for myself I have attained an old age by which I was enabled to fulfil the requirements of the *S*âstras, and thus lead a life of the third order after I left public life.

Now my health is failing fast, and to finish the whole I have made up my mind to enter into the fourth order or Âsrama—namely, that of Sannayâsin. Thereby I shall attain that stage in life when I shall be free from all the cares and anxieties of this world, and shall have nothing to do with my present circumstances in life.

After leading a public life for more than sixty years, I think there is nothing left for me to desire except the life of a Sannayâsin, which will enable my Âtman (self) to be one with Paramâtman (highest self), as shown to us by the enlightened of old. When this is accomplished a man is free from births and rebirths; and what can I wish more than that which will free me from births and rebirths, and give me means to attain Moksha (freedom)?

My learned friend, in a few days I shall be a Sannayâsin, and thus there will be a total change of life. I shall no more be able to address you in this style, so I send you this letter to convey my best wishes for your success in life, and my regards, which you so well deserve.

After this, as you have so well said in your note, you and I will be not two persons, and as the Âtman which, being all-pervading, is one, there is total absence of duality. I shall end this note with the same words which you have mentioned, *Gn*âtvâ Deva*m* sarvapâsâpahâni*h*: When God has been known, all fetters fall.

I heard no more of him except indirectly, when his son sent me a copy of the Bhagavad-gîtâ as a present from his father, who was no longer Gaurî-*s*ankara then, but Sa*kk*idânanda, that is, the Supreme Spirit, i. e. he "who is, who perceives, and is blessed."

It would be a mistake to imagine that a life such as was lived by Gaurî-*s*ankara is usual in modern India. On the contrary, it is now quite exceptional, and Gaurî-*s*ankara was in every respect an exceptional character. Still we must guard against a mistake made by many biographers, who represent their hero as standing alone on a high pedestal without any other people around him with whom he could be compared. We have of late had a number of biographies that would make us believe that in England great men differed by their whole stature from their contemporaries. It is but seldom, however, that we find one man a whole head taller in physical stature than the majority; and so it is in intellectual and moral height also. It is true that it is the head that makes the whole difference, and sometimes a very great difference, still we must never forget that, as a mountain peak seldom stands up by itself, even our greatest men are surrounded in history by their equals, and should be measured accordingly.

Thus in our case, though in Gaurî-*s*ankara we

see a rare union of the man of the world and the man out of the world, of the Prime Minister and the philosopher, it so happens that there were several other statesmen living at the same time who, if they had not actually become hermits, were, all their life, devoted students and followers of the Vedânta. The Minister of the neighbouring state of Junagadh, Gokulaji Zâlâ, who had likewise made his way from poverty to the highest place in his little kingdom, was all his life devoted to the study of the Vedânta. He was the personal friend of Gaurî-*sankara*, and in the reports of the Political Agent he is spoken of as the equal of Gaurî-*sankara*.* Lord Lytton conferred on him the title of Râo Bahâdur, in recognition of his loyal conduct and services. When he died, in 1878, too young to have become a Sannyâsin, it was said that "having done his task, he became, through the true self-knowledge, free from the three forces—casual, subtile, and gross—which disguise the Self, and that his Self, absorbed in the highest Self, became all happiness, just as space, enclosed in a vessel, becomes one with infinite space and force, as soon as the vessel is broken." Everywhere we come across the same Vedântic thoughts in India, though, no doubt,

* See "A Sketch of the Life of Gokulaji Zâlâ and of the Vedânta." By Manassukharâma Sûryarâma Tripâthi. 1881.

under various forms, according to the comprehension of different classes, but in their essence they all mean the same. Gokulaji himself, if we may judge by his biographer, was an assiduous student of the Vedânta all his life, perhaps more even than Gaurî-*s*ankara had been; and, while the latter rejoiced more in the ancient abrupt Vedântic utterances of the Upanishads, Gokulaji had evidently taken an interest in the modern Vedânta also, which enters more minutely into many of the problems which are but started or hinted at in the ancient Upanishads.

In the case of the two Prime Ministers of Bhavnagar and Junagadh there can be little doubt that the Vedântic spirit which filled their minds and guided their steps in life was drawn from a study of the classical works in which that ancient philosophy has been preserved to us. They were Vedântists, as even with us Prime Ministers may be Platonists or Darwinians. But the same philosophical spirit has entered into the language of the people also, into their proverbs and popular maxims, into their laws and poetry. If people, instead of saying "Know thyself," can only say "Know Âtman by Âtman" (know self by self) they are reminded at once of the identity of the ordinary and higher Self. If they meet with people who called themselves Âtmârâma, i.e. self-pleased, they are easily led on to see that the name was really meant for delighting in the Self, i. e. God; if they are taught that he who sees himself in all creatures, and all creatures in himself is a self-sacrificer and obtains the heavenly kingdom, they learn at least that this Self is meant for something more than the material body or the Ego, though it can no doubt be used in that sense also.

This Vedânta spirit pervades the whole of India. It is not restricted to the higher classes, or to men so exceptional as the Prime Minister of Bhavnagar. It lives in the very language of the people, and is preached in the streets and in the forests by mendicant Saints. Even behind the coarse idol-worship of the people some Vedântic truth may often be discovered. The "Sayings of Râmak*ri*sh*n*a," which I lately published ("Râmak*ri*sh*n*a, His Life and Sayings," 1898), are steeped in Vedântic thought, and the life-spring of the reforms inaugurated by such men as Rammohun Roy, Debendranâth Tagore, and Keshub Chunder Sen, must be sought for in the Vedântic Upanishads, though quickened, no doubt, by the spirit of the New Testament.

How omnipresent the influence of the old Vedânta is, even in the lower strata of Indian society, I can, perhaps, show best if I repeat here a story which I have told once before, the story of a poor little girl and her boyish husband. I came to hear that story through her friends who were the friends of Keshub Chunder Sen. We must try to understand, first of all, that it is possible in India for a girl of nine and a boy of twelve to fall in love and to be married, or, rather, to be betrothed. To us such a state of things seems most unnatural; but as long as the custom prevails and is looked upon with favour rather than with disapproval, we can hardly blame a young peasant boy and a still younger peasant girl for following the example set them by their father, mother, and all their friends. That hearts so young are capable of mutual affection and devotion we know from the biographies of some of our own most distinguished men. Nay, we are told by the people of India that the years of their boyish love form the happiest years of their life. As a rule, these young couples remain for some time with their relations—they are like brother and sister; and as they grow up they have the feeling that, like their father and mother, brothers and sisters, husband and wife also are given, not chosen, and the idea that the bonds of their betrothal could ever be severed never enters their minds. The custom itself is no doubt both objectionable and mischievous, and those who have laboured to get it abolished by law deserve our strongest sympathy. All I wish to say here is that we must not make an innocent, ignorant couple, living in an Indian village, responsible for the perversity of a whole nation.

How perverse a nation can be may be seen from an Indian newspaper calling itself *The Indian Nation*, which first denies that Hindu widows are unhappy, and then adds "that, according to Hindu ideas, they ought to be unhappy, because the end of life is not happiness, nor the gratification of dreams, but the regulation, or, if possible, the extinction of them." The widow's life, we are told, was not meant to be joyful, nor should it be rendered joyful or useful, because Hindu ethics are not utilitarian like ours.

These two, *S*rîmatî and her husband Kedar Nâth, were as happy as children all day long; but what is even more surprising than their premature marriage is the premature earnestness with which they looked on life. Their thoughts were engaged on questions which with us would seem but rarely to form the subject of conversation, even of far more mature couples. They felt dissatisfied with their religion which, much as we hear about it in Indian newspapers, occupies after all a very small portion only of the daily life of a poor Hindu family. Their priest may come to say a few prayers before their uncouth idol, provided they possess one, there may be some popular rather than religious festivals to attend, and charitable contributions may be extorted by the priests even from those who have barely enough to eat themselves. They wear their sectarian mark on the forehead, and they may repeat a few simple prayers learnt from their mothers. But of religion, in our sense of the word, they know little indeed. Even when there is a sacred book for their own form of faith, Vedas, Purâ*n*as, or Tantras, they probably have never seen or handled it. They are surrounded, however, by temples and idols, and repulsive idolatrous practices are apt to sicken the heart and to excite doubts even in the least inquisitive minds. Thus when *S*rîmatî's young husband arrived at the conclusion that stones could not be gods (nay, in their hideousness, not even symbols of the Godhead), he took refuge in the Vedânta as preached by Keshub Chunder Sen. This was a bold step. But when he told his young wife what had happened to him, and explained to her his reasons, serious as the consequences of such a step were in India, she, as a faithful and devoted wife, at once followed his example. Even then their creed was indeed very simple. It was not pure Vedânta, it was rather devotional Vedânta-Bhakti, a belief in a phenomenal and personal God, not yet in the Godhead that lends substance and reality to all individual beings, whether gods or men. They held that God was one, without a second, that He existed in the beginning and created the universe. They believed Him to be intelligent, infinite, benevolent, eternal, governor of the universe, all-knowing, all-powerful, the refuge of all, devoid of parts, immutable, self-existent, and beyond all comparison. They also believed that in worshipping Him, and Him alone, they could obtain the highest good in this life and in the next, and that true worship consisted in loving Him and doing His will. There is not much heresy, it would seem, in such a simple creed, but to adopt it meant for the young husband and his wife degradation and complete social isolation. They might easily have kept up an appearance of orthodoxy, while holding in their hearts those simple, pure, and enlightened convictions. The temptation was great, but they resisted. The families to which she and her husband belonged occupied a highly respected position in Hindu society, which in India is fortunately quite compatible with extreme poverty. Much as both she and her husband had been loved and respected before, they were now despised, avoided, excommunicated. Even the allowance which they had received from their family was ordered to be reduced to a minimum, and in order to fit himself to earn an independent livelihood, the husband had to enter as a student in one of the

Government colleges, while his little wife had to look after their small household. Soon there came a new trial. Her husband's father, who had renounced his son when he joined Keshub Chunder Sen's church, died broken-hearted, and the duty of performing the funeral rites (*S*râddha) fell on his son. To neglect to perform these rights is considered something awful, because it is supposed to deprive the departed of all hope of eternal life. The son was quite ready to perform all that was essential in such rites, but he declared that he would never take part in any of the usual idolatrous ceremonies. In spite of the prayers of his relatives and the protestations of the whole village, he would not yield. He fled the very night that the funeral ceremony was to take place, accompanied again by no one except his brave little wife. Thereupon his father's brothers stopped all allowances due to him, and he was left with eight rupees per month to support his wife and mother. *S*rîmatî however managed, with this small pittance, to maintain not only herself and her husband but her husband's mother also, who had become insane, his little sister, and a nurse. Under these changed circumstances her husband found it impossible to continue his career at the Presidency College, and had to migrate to Dacca to prosecute his studies there. Here they all lived together again, and though they were sometimes almost starving, *S*rîmatî considered these years the happiest of her life. She herself tried to perfect her education by attending an Adult Female School, and so rapid was her progress, that on one occasion she was chosen to read an address to Lord Northbrook when he visited the school at Dacca.

The rest of their lives was not very eventful. The husband, after a time, secured a small income; but their life was always a struggle. *S*rîmatî, blessed with healthy children, thought that she had all that her heart desired, though she deeply felt the unkindness of their relatives. Her servants loved her and would never leave her, and when her husband complained of certain irregularities in the household and thought she was too lenient to her maids, she would but sigh and say: "Why should I lose patience, and thereby my peace of mind? Is it not better that I should suffer a little by their conduct than that they should be unhappy!" Her love of her children was most ardent. Yet her highest desire was always the happiness of her husband. She twined round him, as her friends used to say, like a creeper, but it was often the creeper that had to give strength to him and uphold him in his many trials and unfulfilled aspirations. Religion was the never-failing support for both of them, and their conversation constantly turned on the unseen life here and hereafter. The life which they lived together may seem to us uneventful, uninteresting, unsatisfying; but it was not so to them. This quiet couple, breathing the keen, wholesome air of poverty, and drinking from the well of homely life, performing their daily round of duty in the village which had been the home of their ancestors, were happy and perfectly satisfied with their lot on earth. When at last the wife's health began to fail, young and happy as she was, she was quite willing to go. She complained but little on her sick-bed, and her only fear was lest she might disturb her husband's slumber and deprive him of the rest which was so necessary for him. She watched and prayed, and when the end came she looked at him whom she had loved from her early childhood, and quietly murmured: "O, All-merciful" (Dayâmaya), and passed away.

Thus she lived and died: a true child-wife, pure as a child, devoted as a wife, and always yearning for that Spirit whom she had sought for, if, haply, she might feel after Him and find Him. And surely He was not far from her, nor she from Him!

THE END.

INDEX